D0825581

The
Smart
Woman's
Guide

to
Career Success

The
Smart
Woman's
Guide
to
Career Success

By
Janet Hauter

CAREER PRESS
180 Fifth Ave., P.O. Box 34
Hawthorne, NJ 07507
1-800-CAREER-1
201-427-0229 (outside U.S.)
FAX: 201-427-2037

THE SMART WOMAN'S GUIDE TO CAREER SUCCESS
ISBN 1-56414-056-3, $11.95
Cover design by Dean Johnson Design, Inc.
Printed by Book-mart Press

To order this title by mail, please include price as noted above, $2.50 handling per order, and $1.00 for each book ordered. Send to: Career Press, Inc., 180 Fifth Ave., P.O. Box 34, Hawthorne, NJ 07507

Or call toll-free 1-800-CAREER-1 (Canada: 201-427-0229) to order using VISA or MasterCard, or for further information on books from Career Press.

Library of Congress Cataloging-in-Publication Data

Hauter, Janet, 1942-
    The smart woman's guide to career success / by Janet
Hauter.
        p. cm.
    Includes bibliographical references and index.
    ISBN 1-56414-056-3 : $11.95
    1. Vocational guidance for women. 2. Sex discrimination in
employment. 3. Sexual harassment of women. 4. Career
development. I. Title.
HF5382.6.H38   1993
650.14'082--dc20   93-7560
                                                              CIP

Dedication

This book is dedicated to the five individuals who challenged and supported me to "stretch" every one of my God-given talents to the max:

My zealot mother, Verna Wojcik, who is my staunchest and most unrelenting coach and mentor; my husband, John, whose faith in me and my gifts has challenged, encouraged and nurtured me by giving me the freedom to be who I really am; my sons, John, Brad and Stephen, who directly and indirectly, willingly and unwillingly stretch my patience, my comfort levels, my energies, my abilities and skills to simultaneously serve *and* lead in areas that I could never have chosen by myself. I humbly thank you all.

Contents

Introduction

In the middle of a favorable salary review, I remember surprising a former boss with my reaction. He had just awarded me a generous increase—one I knew I had earned in spades. I simply smiled. Clearly perplexed, he exclaimed, "I expected you to be overjoyed. What is it you really want?"

My answer was simple: "More! More responsibility. More independence. More mobility. More direct reports. More income. More!"

My directness may have startled him, but it also impressed him. Not only did he answer my eagerness to develop professionally by challenging me with a new project, but he also scheduled another salary review within six months, instead of the traditional year.

You must have the same eagerness to develop and advance as a professional—or you wouldn't have bought this book. But how often have you been surprised that your efforts didn't bring the rewards you expected? If you're like me, too many! At a time when our sheer numbers in the workplace make us a force to be reckoned with, why do so many hard-working, motivated career women still feel "on the outside looking in"?

9

Because as women, many of us are, quite literally, "strangers in a strange land"! When we stepped into the world of business, most of us were unaware that we would be expected to adopt the values of an entirely new—and often very foreign—business culture.

How important is culture? If you were planning to travel to France, you'd probably make an effort to learn enough about the language and customs to avoid appearing *gauche*, as well as to get more enjoyment from your trip. As women planning to travel through the ranks of a business world created by men, we face a similar cultural "gap." We may speak the same language—although even that is debatable! But culturally, we might as well be from the moon! It's high time we became "fluent" in the rules and customs we need to become real contenders.

No matter how lofty your goals or how limited your progress to date, the sooner you master the nuances of business culture, the sooner you'll be able to maximize your career success using your innate skills as a woman and as an individual. I hope you'll let this book be your guide.

During my years as a trainer, career counselor, manager and, finally, president of my own company, I've encountered most of the roadblocks and glass ceilings that confound even the most focused professional women. What distresses me is that many women appear to be opting out of the struggle or scaling back their career goals by not cultivating the full measure of their abilities.

If you are one of these women, I urge you to reconsider. The loss of your potential will weaken us all.

In the course of a career that sometimes felt like a roller coaster ride, I've tasted success and been frustrated by injustices that have threatened my achievement, such as discrimination and exploitation. I've also made plenty of my own mistakes. But along the way, I discovered some strategies that helped me navigate successfully as a woman in the world of business. I'd like to share them with you.

As women, we bring our own unique set of qualities with us to work. Sensitive and empathetic by nature, we tend to be good listeners and often work well with others. Because we're frequently required to balance a hectic home life with a full-time job, we've become skilled at juggling an inordinate number of projects simultaneously. But while these qualities may be valued—they rarely lead to the kind of power, influence, salary increases and professional advancement we seek in what is still very much a man's world.

Whether you're part of a traditional, highly structured corporate environment—or small company in which everyone wears several hats, the business culture that drives it was forged by men out of the hierarchy and team ethic bred in boys from a very early age. And they continue to dominate, simply because they made up the rules!

As little girls, we were raised to have very different values. So it's no wonder that today most of us continue to plug away—unaware that the qualities we value in ourselves put us at a distinct disadvantage on the corporate playing field! Well, we may not be the "home team," but we have every opportunity to win in business, now and in the years ahead.

You may be in a nonmanagerial position or aiming for the top job. Or you may have launched a solo career as a home-based entrepreneur. Even if you're just starting out, with only a vague idea of where you want your career to go, your ultimate success is in understanding and adapting to business culture. Once you master the rules and customs, you'll be able to "read" the power structure and move ahead with real authority.

For those of you with the vision and fortitude to push ahead no matter what the obstacles, this book will provide strategic tactics that should make the battle considerably easier to win using new avenues of influence you haven't previously explored.

The Smart Woman's Guide

But this book is especially dedicated to the many capable women who feel discouraged by a vague sense of not clicking—whether they work in large corporations, small start-ups or home-based entrepreneurial ventures.

In *Work of Her Own* (1992), Susan Albert found that working women cope with career frustration in a variety of ways. In interviews with 80 women who changed their career path, she found:

- 31 percent stayed in the workplace, but sought less stressful work.
- 31 percent opted for self-employment.
- 22 percent became full-time homemakers.
- 9 percent went back to school full-time, so they could retrain for careers in which they thought they'd have more control over their work.
- 7 percent, who had enough money to live on, simply quit working.

While there are almost as many alternative workstyles and lifestyles as there are individual women, the important thing is that many opportunities exist for each one of us to fully develop our unique potential. Throughout this book, I'll encourage you to dream big dreams. But I'll also give you tools—from questionnaires to practical step-by-step strategies—to help you plan and carry out the career goals you identify.

I am truly excited about the potential for every woman to become a leader in the years ahead. *Workforce 2000: Work and Workers for the 21st Century* (June, 1987), a document produced by the Hudson Institute, projects that woman will soon dominate the work force in number for the first time in history. Clearly, the best is yet to be. Don't let business culture be your only stumbling block.

Read on.

1

The business persona: Tuning into an organization's culture

To begin to understand the dynamic world of business, let's look at art.

If you've ever stepped in close to examine a landscape rendered by an artist using a post-Impressionistic technique called pointillism, you probably found it easier to see the thousands of point-sized specks of paint on the canvas than the scene they are meant to compose. But when you stepped back, the points "magically" blended to create a single and complete impression.

So it is with the culture that identifies and drives your organization, company or business enterprise. Many, often subtle, "point-sized" rules and customs are picked up and repeated by a group of employees—until their actions "blend" into a collective attitude. Within this community, the accepted culture—even if it is unconsciously accepted by many—defines how each individual should think, act and make decisions. Ultimately, it will determine which individuals are promoted.

The phenomenon of culture

None of us is a stranger to culture. In fact, without a framework of rules for understanding and operating in our everyday world, life would be chaos. There is no formal classroom for teaching the many manners and mores we practice. We pick up what we need—from rules about personal space to social manners—from our experiences in the course of living our lives.

If we were to travel to another state or another country, the rules might be significantly different. In fact, we become so invested in our own way of doing things that we are often disturbed—sometimes even insulted—by the behavior exhibited by people from different cultures, generations or parts of the world.

In the world of work, it is much the same. Defined as "a system of informal rules that spell out how people are to behave most of the time" in *Corporate Cultures: The Rites and Rituals of Corporate Life*, by Terrence E. Deal and Allen A. Kennedy, "corporate culture" became a darling concept of the '80s. Today, the definition is still valid, but I'd rename the concept for the '90s. These days, *business culture* reaches beyond the bounds of large corporations to apply to a growing number of start-ups and home-based businesses.

As you "travel" from company to company, you will enter the equivalent of mini-countries, each with its own way of doing things. Any seasoned professional can tell you, an approach that works in one culture can have disastrous effects in another.

A word about the gender gap

As women, we must be prepared to deal with cultural dynamics on two levels. The foundation for the unique cultural traits found within individual companies is often a rigid organizational structure—or hierarchy—based on the military and sports-ethics men were raised to value. As women, we were raised with very different values. The gap between our actions and the values of the hierarchy is often our professional undoing. We'll explore this complicated organizational structure in more detail later.

For now, let's focus on the unique qualities that distinguish individual businesses—whether large organizations, companies or home-based enterprises—from each other.

Reading the clues

There are many clues to the deeply held cultural beliefs at the heart of any business. If you're tempted to discard many of these nuances I'm about to introduce you to as trivial and insignificant, resist. You'll see that what is subtle can often be quite powerful.

When you combine all the cultural clues, you'll have important information you can use to guide you to a job in an environment that will nourish—rather than starve—your unique abilities and goals. Let's begin by taking a tour of your company.

1. Business identity: The face the world sees

A company is as multifaceted as any person you know. For example, each company creates a public identity—an image or face it shows the outside world—that may or may not accurately reflect its private life.

A company that proudly boasts that its customers are always "number one" may appeared to be people-oriented. But its employees may be receiving another message: "So, you will always be second-best." Not surprisingly, these employees often find it difficult to take pride in their work and may even skimp on quality standards.

In this type of "us-and-them" environment, you might find many cultures—by department, hierarchy or even by job—that ultimately fragment the productivity of the entire enterprise.

2. The building: Are looks everything?

Well, not everything. But you should be able to tell as much from the appearance of a company as you can from a person's appearance on first meeting.

As you approach your company, take a few extra moments to study the architecture of the building you're about to enter. Is it conservative and understated or colorful and dramatic? Does it seem to blend into its setting or "beg" to be noticed—day and night? Does its appearance seem appropriate to its business?

One Fortune 500 company I pass regularly is set, like a jewel, atop a hill overlooking hundreds of manicured acres just off a major interstate. The grounds include a strategically placed lake populated with ducks and geese. There is no doubt that this company made as much of an "ego" investment as monetary in creating this monument.

Yet, not a year after the building was fully staffed and functional, 30 percent of the new employees were laid off! It doesn't take much analysis to determine that this company is more interested in investing in an impressive public image than in protecting human "capital."

3. The entry way: How warm is the reception?

Now, we're inside. How do you feel standing in the entry way? Is it aesthetic or simply functional? Does it feel like a warm, welcoming place—or a cold, impersonal waiting room?

When one of my clients, a dentist, told me he was mystified by what he felt was an exaggerated level of anxiety in his patients, I scheduled a visit. I only had to step into his reception area myself to solve the mystery.

After checking in with the receptionist—who never looked up again—behind a glass wall, patients were expected to find a seat on one of the uncomfortable metal chairs. There were a few magazines (each more than three months old) available to help kill the time. But there was no music to kill the sound of the dentist's drill in what sounded like a torture chamber within.

This business was definitely not sensitive to its customers! It's not difficult to understand why most patients were feeling anxious by the time they saw the dentist. In fact, I'm surprised many of them got that far!

4. Business literature: Can you judge it by its cover?

As you continue to look around, take a moment to review the printed literature on display. What types of materials are available? How does each piece look and feel? If the company's brochures are extravagant, are they in sync with the surroundings?

How do they read? Does the company use its printed literature as propaganda—or is the language informative and sensitive to the specific needs of its customers? How do these materials compare to the look and language of classified advertising bent on "seducing" employees instead of clients?

Recently, I picked up some brochures produced by a successful consulting organization. At first, I was dismayed to find that this group of young executives had used these pieces to create a pedestal-in-print for their business. They came across as snooty and socially competitive.

Did the brochure put off potential customers? Not likely! They knew their market. The competitive companies they are courting are just as interested in proving to competitors that they can afford such high-priced services as they are in gaining a competitive advantage!

Here's a distinctly different approach: A successful plastic surgeon produced a very elegant brochure featuring the image of an attractive person embossed in gold on a background of royal purple. The only "message" on the cover was the name of the surgeon's clinic.

Of course the brochure had to "feel" expensive to underline the surgeon's expertise. But by focusing on an individual—"haloed" in gold embossing—the surgeon very eloquently called attention to the fact that he is dedicated to the unique needs of each patient.

5. Pictures: They speak a thousand words

As you move away from the reception area, down the halls and into the meeting rooms of the company, take note of the artwork around you.

Does there seem to be a theme? If most of the artwork is modern—perhaps even *avant-garde*—the company may be ahead of its time, as well. If the art seems to have a retrospective theme—showcasing its founders, for example—you can expect the company to be traditional and conservative.

Often, the artwork in the lobby or reception area also provides insight into what the organization is interested in becoming. For example, a small Midwestern manufacturing company reserves a key position in its lobby for a picture frame holding a simple sentence inscribed in calligraphy: "This space is reserved for the Malcolm Baldridge award." No visitor can miss the message: The reference to the award to corporations who satisfy a stringent set of performance criteria clearly indicates that the company is serious about quality. The irony is that there is no such sign on the manufacturing floor to motivate the workers with the power to enhance product quality. By focusing on the showpiece, company executives are apparently hoping for the best. The goal then remains unidimensional—unshared by the very people who can make the dream reality.

6. People: Taking things seriously

OK, down to the nitty-gritty. Who are the people behind the company's facade? Are they the heart and soul of the

19

organization, or do they tend to be transient, short-timers? There are a number of clues:

Dress code. In most companies, office employees don't wear a uniform. Or do they? Take a close look at the way the people you pass in the halls are dressed. Are there similarities in style—no matter how subtle—that seem to make a collective statement about the entire organization?

Can you identify a hierarchy that separates executives, with very expensive suits and jewelry, from less expensively dressed administrative staff?

Age. Make a note of the average age of the people you see. If the majority of people are young, the culture is more likely to be aggressive and fast-paced. Conversely, if the people tend to be older, there may be an overall tendency to act cautiously and deliberately as a company.

Pace. By now, you will have gotten a sense for how quickly people are moving. If the people you see seem to have a sense of urgency, it's safe to assume that the company promotes tight deadlines and short lead times for the completion of projects. If the pace is sultry, and people seem to cluster for long chats, perhaps little is being accomplished or their is a long approval cycle that keep projects stuck in channels.

Attitude. In other words, how happy do employees *seem*? Do people at all levels laugh spontaneously and often? Or are people at lower levels always looking over their shoulders to avoid being heard by others with more political clout?

The grapevine. In candid conversation, what do employees say about the work, their bosses, the company's leadership? Are they outspoken about the need for better communication and higher salaries? Or do they seem to be evangelical about the company team?

Teamwork. Does the organization appear to pull together as a team? Or is teamwork given plenty of lip service, but very little support?

You might expect a male-dominated organization to function like a winning sports team. But this is rarely the case. Managers may not act like effective coaches, giving individuals team members the strategic information they need to "play their positions" to the best of their abilities. While there is little doubt that the ultimate goal is winning, many companies may not value winning *together*.

One CEO had trouble understanding why employees throughout her company always seemed so hungry for information. She went as far as to openly berate their curiosity, referring to them "information junkies" in her executive meetings. Yet, this same CEO changed the corporate mission statement each quarter. In fact, most information about the company's actions was withheld—so employees never knew what was going on.

Clearly, the executive message was that information is power. By keeping the majority of employees in an information vacuum, the CEO succeeded in keeping them powerless. But she also inadvertently created just the type of employee she was critical of—dependent and wary. It became a self-fulfilling prophecy.

Recognition. How are employees recognized? Are they rewarded only for their performance as workers—or are they also valued as people?

One company made a practice of sending each employee a floral arrangement on his or her birthday. Enter a change in leadership—and then a recession. Of course, the birthday floral arrangements were among the first items to be cut from the budget. But when the company made no effort to replace this personal attention with a more cost-effective gesture, it may have communicated the message that an employee's personal value is expendable.

When a company supports a casual day and then abruptly takes it away—or allows employees to bring food into their departments only to withdraw the privilege—people are bound to perceive management as more restrictive and controlling than if the privilege had been denied from the outset.

History: Is it worth repeating? You know the adage: "History repeats itself." So look for trends in the way a company makes decisions, resolves problems and manages crises today. You may have a pretty good view of the future.

Also learn the employees' history with the company. Did they complete a trainee program? Has their progress been rapid or slow? What is the average tenure of the employees in different departments? What makes them stay so long—or leave so soon? Your questions can help you gather the information you need to take an objective view of the company using a composite of the experiences of many individuals.

Vision: Walking the talk. How does the company describe its vision of the future? How does the company plan to make that vision reality? Most important of all, does it "walk the talk" today?

If you can't find a statement of vision in the annual report or other printed materials, ask others if they've heard about how upper management is charting the company's long-term course.

7. Help-wanted ads: Classified information

Pay special attention to the company's classified advertising. What words and visual images are used to attract and court potential employees? Is there a lot of talk about benefits and the potential for growth, or is the best news the "competitive" salaries (which may not be all that competitive, after all). Are the ads large and airy, with plenty of white space? Or are abbreviated descriptions shoe-horned into the smallest (and least expensive) space? Few ads give more than the perfunctory knowledge, skills and task description—a flat picture of a very dynamic reality.

What makes a successful culture?

Generally, it creates an atmosphere in which people are encouraged and rewarded for achieving results—rather than tripped up by unproductive office politics, empire-building and petty conflicts. Specifically, it's wise to look for the following:

- Goals and plans that are clearly understood by every employee—and used as the basis for every-day work.
- A commitment to making accurate and complete information immediately available to the people who need it.
- Teamwork within departments to motivate groups of individuals to cooperate in reaching—and even exceeding—organizational goals.
- Clear relationships between jobs, so tasks are not performed redundantly across the organization.
- Management go-ahead for employees to use their own initiative and ask plenty of questions.
- Results-oriented performance standards in which goals and specific results are clearly defined and communicated, so each employee can effectively measure and monitor his or her own progress.

- Dynamic planning that is responsive to change, yet straightforward and easy to carry out.
- Competitive compensation that is tied to performance, not politics.
- Opportunities for each employee to grow and develop as an individual, as well as a professional.

And watch out for...

There are five "subversive" influences you should avoid at all costs. Not only are these management practices unhealthy for you as an individual—but, should *you* survive, the company that promotes them is likely to fail. If you discover one or more of the following demons, run—and don't look back!

- "Hidden agendas" that camouflage or conceal the real issues.
- A hierarchy in which status is clearly valued over quality.
- Restrictive control over employees.
- Excessive turnover, absenteeism and tardiness.
- Overt attempts to foster fear and distrust among employees.

Making sense out of chaos

If, after all this evaluation, you still don't have a clear picture of the company in question, you're not alone. In *Thriving on Chaos*, Tom Peters shows us that chaos—not productivity—seems to be the norm in many companies today. In a disorganized and changing environment, many employees feel less fulfilled. As women, we can be especially vulnerable to a chaotic work environment and may react by becoming anxious, apathetic or simply disenchanted. But our attitude toward chaos is the key to maximizing our performance.

Men tend to tolerate chaos and uncertainty because they are driven to achieve their personal goals. But as women, we can bring real value to a disorganized environment by creating competitive collaborations.

A woman's touch

After all, we do it all the time in our families! If you've ever pulled off a successful Thanksgiving dinner for your family and relatives, you should already be an expert at getting a diverse group of individuals to cooperate in achieving a single goal! If we know how to appeal to the character and ability of each individual family member as wives, mothers or daughters we can make the best use of the skills and abilities of a diverse team as co-workers and managers.

Using the skills you've already demonstrated—and trusting your inherent abilities as a woman—you *can* find order and effectiveness in chaos.

The journey is the reward

Like anything worth pursing, career success is a process—a journey. It's bound to have its peaks and its valleys, its shortcuts and its dead-ends. You can stumble blindly around each bend in the road. Or you can use all the knowledge and skills at your command to navigate toward your final destination.

Am I asking you to have your antenna at full power? Absolutely! But the farther you travel, the easier it will be—and the more you'll know about who you are and where you're going. With practice, patience and plenty of perseverance, there is no end to the personal and professional rewards you can find on the career road ahead.

2

The evolution of organizational culture

Work is nothing new to women. From the beginning of time, we've pulled our weight—as primary care givers at home, side by side with men during planting and harvest and in factories and stores. In recent years, we've been moving through the executive ranks of companies and launching successful enterprises of our own.

Yet I expect our contributions to date to pale beside what women will be able to achieve in the decade ahead. Changing demographics indicate that soon we'll be members of the *majority* in the work force—overtaking men in number for the first time in history. If we're prepared with the skills and business savvy to tap the many opportunities and career challenges that will present themselves, we should be able to make a mark as no other generation of women has.

But how did we arrive at this spot? Because history is always an enlightening guide to future moves, let's take a moment to review our evolution.

The Agricultural Age

Most of us have ancestors who came to this country as immigrants. Short on savings and often at a disadvantage in terms of language and learning, many turned to farming. It wasn't an easy life for men who performed most tasks by hand or with horses or mules—or for the women who performed at least as many tasks by hand, in addition to creating and managing the "human resources."

The prairie "corporation"

You might liken the farm family to a small corporation. Fundamentally, it was a team of people working toward the common and critical goal: survival. Each family member was assigned tasks based on his or her age, capability, physical strength and stamina. With the years, came "promotion"—and more demanding tasks.

In our dual role as farmhand and primary care giver, women shared in daily and seasonal chores—and bore full responsibility for cooking, cleaning and mending. We also directed much of the work and care of the family team. In fact, you might say the frontier spawned the first female "corporate managers."

Motivating "employees" wasn't much of a problem, even though the workday typically lasted from sunrise to sundown and the work was physically exacting and repetitious. If there was food on the table each day, there was "profitability" in this simple community lifestyle.

The Industrial Age

As we grew into the Industrial Age, many able-bodied men left the farm for higher wages in factories. The advent of the assembly line made mass production possible for a range of manufacturers. Technology was the key to providing the "muscle" and speed to support increased volume. Ultimately, it would shape the structure of our modern organizations.

Serving the master machine

It wasn't long before the machine upstaged the worker. In the minds of company officials, workers were expendable slaves to technology. With a never-ending pool of immigrant labor to draw from, they began to set up "sweatshops" and steadily increase production quotas to meet the rising demand of a new nation of consumers. Although women played a role—primarily as seamstresses—this was a man's world.

Dependent on a machine, rather than on other workers, men often performed specialized tasks alone or as part of a small, loosely woven group.

The rise of "position power"

If there was little value in being a worker, there was real prestige and power in evolving authority positions. The Industrial Age gave birth to an imposing, autocratic figure—the factory "boss." Using the language barrier and brute force to keep English-speaking and immigrant workers in line, the boss used a military style of management to impose harsh standards and discipline on an already devalued work force. It was inevitable that unions would be formed to protect workers who couldn't protect themselves from what are now illegal practices. But even with intervention from union bosses, working conditions continued to erode morale. It wasn't long before unions that had begun fighting for more humane hours and wages turned to defending the actions of an increasingly discontented and unruly work force.

Although machines boosted production, the nature of the factory work was—like farming—semi-skilled and repetitious.

But unlike farming, the emphasis among workers was not on working for the prosperity of the family unit or team, but on keeping productivity down to protect the group from ever-increasing production quota systems. New workers were chided by established group members for producing "too well." Any increase in production would mean a new, higher quota for the entire group the following day. This may well have been the introduction of employee sabotage.

Enter: Rosie the Riveter

It took World War II to bring women back into the working ranks. As men left their jobs to go to war, women stepped in to fill their jobs.

"Rosie the Riveter" soon became the popular persona for competent working women who extended their roles as care giver to include a full-time—if short-term—factory career.

But an interesting thing happened. Women entering what they thought would be a cooperative environment, in the spirit of the farm and family, found that competition was the new name of the game. And much to the surprise of the men who hired them, they rose to the challenge.

For the first time, women were promoted for their efforts—rising from worker to group leader to supervisor and even into management positions. With this first taste of career success and its financial reward, many vowed to continue working—even after the men returned. Women discovered a new dimension of themselves and the dis- covery brought self-confidence.

The Information Age

With each passing decade, technology has been re- defined until, today, there is a computer on nearly every desk. Individuals and companies have the power to boost productivity to a level not dreamed of even a decade ago.

But productivity hasn't always been accompanied by efficiency. In fact, all too many times the price of unrelent- ing innovation has been chaos.

Those invincible '80s: More is better

Early on, each new advance in what could only be described as a revolution in business technology made many companies feel invincible.

In a mania of mergers, acquisitions and leveraged buyouts, large organizations competed fiercely for small companies—even those with little or no relation to their core business. Accumulation became an end in itself. Corporate decision-makers (and I use the term loosely) seemed to lose their heads in a celebration of the abundance of money and credit. But, after a "no-limits" night on the town, there had to be a morning after.

Near the end of the '80s, companies woke up to find customers turning away from unresponsive policies and service. And technology—the panacea—was promoting chaos by randomly decentralizing the traditional organizational hierarchy.

In some companies, the power to react quickly using technology still fosters management-by-crisis. Others seem to be constantly in flux—introducing an ever-changing array of rules, systems and strategies that work in specific situations, but never seem to work in tandem.

The changing face of business

By bringing power and productivity to the fingertips of individuals in the ranks, technology has seriously undermined the "authority" of traditional hierarchies. In fact, in this dynamic new environment, highly structured systems seem to have the effect of slowing down decision-making and problem-solving.

As a result, business is moving toward an updated design that allows more "local" control and promotes teamwork to ensure responsiveness in a more competitive marketplace.

The customer as "boss"

Companies that lost sight of the needs of customers—and then lost customers—are not likely to make that mistake again in the near future. Most are experimenting with decentralized operations, so they can meet the specific needs of even small pockets of customers.

Wal-Mart sets a good example in the retail world. With hundreds of stores serving as many diverse communities, Wal-Mart could save hundreds of thousands of dollars by purchasing merchandise from a central location and then distributing it to each local store. Instead, corporate headquarters puts each store manager in control.

Local managers stock their shelves with only those products their customers ask for. As a result, customers come to rely on Wal-Mart for faster, better service—giving Wal-Mart an overall competitive edge. What's more, quick service from local suppliers enables store managers to order "just-in-time." For some, this has meant eliminating as much as 25 percent of excess inventory and cutting time spent restocking from six weeks to less than two days!

With insight into how and why organizations have evolved as they have, women can begin to recognize promising opportunities already becoming available in what I'll call the New Organization! Now, more than ever before, we need to tune into the ever-changing business climate—watching, listening, reading and identifying trends—so we'll be ready to participate.

Working in the New Organization

Like many systems born to serve a specific situation, the Industrial Age served its purpose. It's only appropriate that we begin to loosen the grip of its management legacy. Initially, that may mean trading structure for some measure of "chaos." In the New Organization, there will be plenty of opportunity for the employee who can adapt to change and ambiguity and still be highly productive, whether working alone or as part of a close-knit team of professionals.

Diversity: The human denominator

Unlike the Industrial Age, the Information Age values the diversity of its human resources. Discrimination and a rigid hierarchy will give way to a range of work and management styles. While the "good-old-boy" network cloned top managers, right down to the conservative "uniform," the New Organization will see diversity as a catalyst for creativity and innovation.

New management style: Investing in cooperation

Competition is good—even necessary. But we're finding that collaboration is even better. When sales and marketing are involved in jockeying for "internal market share" of staff or budget, it can be easy to lose sight of the real competition—gaining market share outside the company. It's important to focus that competitive energy into collaborative efforts that challenge individuals to join forces to meet goals. In this environment, information is shared and input is encouraged. Even conflict can be the source of information that can be used in development and decision-making.

The changing role of women

The good news is that most of these changes put women ahead of the game. The qualities that were once at odds with the traditional hierarchy—such as our regard for individual contributions and cooperation—are now being acknowledged as strengths that can significantly enhance productivity and performance in the New Organization.

Instead of focusing on the scarcity of win-lose, as men traditionally have, women can show companies how to think in terms of abundance. Rather than launch a single-minded drive to win at any cost, we can use our interpersonal savvy to create a new kind of management style that encourages everyone to stretch his or her abilities. With everyone performing in top form, the winnings will multiply—along with the potential power, recognition, influence and financial rewards for everyone who plays a role.

Here's the challenge: To make our mark in the New Organization, we'll need continuous education, more knowledge, more skill and more ability than ever before in history to keep pace with an ever-changing organization. Education will be the only ticket to promotion.

From survival to full-service

So how far have we come? Many of us are still primary care givers, but these days we have support from technology and a multitude of consumer services designed for the two- income household. With the assistance of professional domestic help, day care, eldercare and a variety of shopping services, we are closer to being able to "do it all"— because so much of *it* is done for us.

One creative entrepreneur answered the many needs of two-income families in an upscale Midwestern suburb by opening one unique day-care/family-care center. Parents are reassured that their children will be cared for in the same *nouveau riche* environment they left at home. These pampered children even nap in cribs imported from Italy!

But the parents are pampered, as well. When they drop off the children, parents may also drop off their dry cleaning and shoes for repair. Some even take a moment or two to order dinner from an exclusive gourmet menu! When they return after work, the children, dry cleaning, shoes and dinner are ready—in one stop.

Sound farfetched? This full-service phenomenon is already here to stay. Yet it's still only a glimmer of what's in store as our lifestyles continue to change to match our creative workstyles.

Opening your window of opportunity

We've come a long way. Rather than work for our own survival or fill in for men in the service of our country, we have new opportunities to shine in our own right. The next six to ten years, with tell the story. But the time to begin preparing is right now.

For the first time in history, the window of opportunity is wide open. And the view is beautiful.

3

Today's work force: Putting opportunity into perspective

So far, I've talked a lot about opportunity. By now you know I want to excite you about the many opportunities that are already appearing on the horizon—and inspire you to take advantage of them. What I don't want to do is to lull you into a false sense of security.

According to my *Webster's Dictionary*, opportunity is "a favorable or promising combination of circumstances. A chance for advancement or improvement." I believe in the power of this concept so much that I want you to make it the cornerstone in your plan for career success. But even with the richest opportunities, success can be downright elusive if you're so caught up in chasing unimportant goals or indulging in self-pity you don't recognize them!

If you're new to the world of work, or simply need a more effective strategy for getting ahead, your understanding of how the game of business is played will put you in line for many opportunities. With the right knowledge and skills, you'll be prepared to capitalize on every "favorable combination of circumstances" that comes your way.

With this in mind, let's begin by stepping back to get some perspective on the "big picture"—the world of work.

The coming demographic explosion

Like a thunderbolt, the opening statement in a report titled *Workforce 2000: Work and Workers for the 21st Century*, published by the Hudson Institute in June 1987, prepared futurists for an impending flash of change on the horizon:

> *"The year 2000 will mark the end of what has been called the American century...The last years of this century are certain to bring new developments in technology, international competition, demography and other factors that will alter the nation's economic and social landscape."*

While the report concentrated on how these significant changes would affect workers in the United States, it's important to recognize that these trends are global. Here are some of the highlights:

- Service industries will soon dominate our national economy. In fact, 90 percent of all new jobs will be created in the service sector. Less than 10 percent are expected to open up in manufacturing.
- Our work force will grow more slowly than it has in past years, and reflect a changing population that is older and predominantly female.
- More women will be working than ever before. More than 60 percent of all women over the age of 16 will be working, representing nearly 48 percent of the national employment count.
- Other minority groups will make a stronger showing. In general, minority groups will nearly double their numbers in the work force to account for 30 percent of all new entrants. Black women will

show the greatest increase, outnumbering black men for the first time. Hispanics also will be present in record numbers, to make up more than 29 percent of the total work force.

- Together, women and other minority groups will comprise a majority in the labor force for the first time in history!

Opportunity at every turn

As members of the new majority, women can expect the gates of opportunity to swing open in nearly every profession. However:

- The technical and sales fields will show the fastest growth for professionals. At an average age of 39, workers will be expected to bring a blend of academic and real-world knowledge to new positions.
- As competition intensifies, higher education will be more important than ever. In fact, having only a high school diploma may put you at a distinct disadvantage if you're building a career. You can expect to spend three times longer looking for a job than competing applicants with a higher education. And once you've landed the job, you may "plateau" early with little or no opportunity for promotion!
- Some 41 percent of new jobs will require a high level of skill and many jobs will be ranked by skill-level rather than by education. By contrast, low-skill jobs will shrink rapidly.

What it all means—for women

Clearly, this demographic shift will have an impact on women. Whether you entered the work force by choice or out of economic necessity, you'll be able to count on the strength of our number in many areas. Expect some significant changes in present "policy." For example:

- The wage gap between men and women should begin to close. Recent statistics indicate that we earn as little as 54 percent of what our male counterparts earn!

- A more comprehensive plan for subsidizing and regulating day care and eldercare will become critical, as we continue to balance work with caring for children as well as aging parents who live in or outside the home.

- Alternative workstyles—such as part-time work and flextime—will be more available. Job-sharing will become more common in many companies as a flexible solution for women—and men—who share comparable skills and want to work part-time. An increasing number of women will create home-based businesses.

- Geographic transfers will decline with the continued rise of two-income families.

- We'll be able do more in less time, so many of us will spend less time at work.

- Companies with offer more benefits to ease stress on two-career families—from on-site cafeterias to parental leaves for both men and women.

- Life-long learning will become an integral part of every job to help workers keep pace with rapid changes in technology.

- More workers will work at home rather than in office environments—often to accomodate children and aging parents.

41

- There will also be an influx of entrepreneurs—those who reject the prototype of the traditional organization to venture out on their own.

Inside the organization of the future

The demographic explosion will also rock the marketplace. To become more responsive to the demands of the *real* boss—the customer—business will have to become leaner, more focused and more aggressive. By leveling multiple layers of management to create a flatter organizational structure, companies will offer workers more challenge—and expect more productivity in return.

Focus on performance

A continued trend toward downsizing to correct the deficits brought on by out-of-control spending in the '80s will lead companies to focus on maximizing the performance of people and technology. As technology is pressed into service to handle more and more complex tasks—the "human resources" will have more time to develop creative solutions using old-fashioned brain power.

"Smarter" products

Technology and creativity will continue to come together to create "smarter" products and services for busy consumers. Already, many of today's cars can analyze their own maintenance needs—telling you when to replace washer fluid or rotate the tires via a diagram on the dashboard.

The mobile employee

You'll trade job security for increased opportunity. Trends indicate that the average American will work in approximately 10 different jobs in at least five different companies before retiring.

"Intrapreneurism"

Small, specialized business units will continue to be born and nurtured within the "safe" confines of many large, established organizations. During the past decade, these *intrapreneurial* ventures brought a dedicated group of employees together to develop innovative new concepts and products. With funding and protection from traditional "thou shalt not" policies, these fledgling businesses have every chance of "growing up" to become independent start-up companies. In the meantime, the parent company has developed a taste for the creative excitement common in smaller companies.

Are you looking for a job or a career?

This is an important distinction. Since we've gotten this far together, I assume that you're interested in building a career. But do your actions and career choices to date reflect that decision?

When you look back over your work history, do you see a series of thoughtful choices that resulted in steady progress toward a defined goal? If so, I applaud you—and encourage you to keep up the good work. But if you find you've simply drifted from job to job, reacting to changes as they occurred, it may be time to do some serious thinking about your future.

What kind of "traveler" are you?

If you begin now to think of your work as a long journey toward an ultimate destination of your choice, you can carefully chart your entire route—from beginning to end. When you embark on any trip, you want to have a pretty good idea of how much time it should take to get to each intermediate stop, so you can stay on schedule. By updating progress according to the route you've mapped out, you won't be as tempted to take side-trips or be delayed for long by roadblocks or detours.

But if you're only looking as far ahead as the next stop—whether it be a promotion or new job—you may not notice when you begin to drift and risk wasting valuable time. Without an ultimate goal in mind, there is little motivation to press on to the next destination.

What inspires you to work?

What qualities do you value in yourself? What prompted your employer to invest in you? Check your current situation against the following.

Ability. What is the unique blend of knowledge, skills and experience you bring to your current job? Take nothing for granted! Even the most subtle quality can be important.

Challenge. How do you actively promote the company's goals through your job. How will you and the company benefit—now and in the long term?

Responsibility. Have you already been rewarded for getting results? How did you get them? Most employers look for a combination of intelligence and practical self-management skills, such as organization and follow-through.

Attitude. Do you take pride in doing a good job? Are you committed to working hard and setting a positive example for others on the staff?

Initiative. Are you known as a creative problem-solver? Or do you wait for instructions at every turn?

Redirecting your efforts

If you're just starting out, changing careers or simply would like to invest more time in examining your personal gifts and career motivations, I suggest you also invest in Naomi Stephan's book, *Finding Your Life Mission*. This is an innovative and comprehensive approach to self-discovery and direction.

You've decided you want to "go for it." Now what? You'll need top-notch skills and experience to compete in your chosen field and job, along with a new approach to getting ahead.

Removing boundaries

As women, we tend to get caught up in the concerns of a very limited "territory" that doesn't reach much further than our own job. The danger in having our noses too close to the grindstone is that we can't look around to see what else is going on. It's time to develop a more expansive view.

Contrary to the way many of us may feel, making active contributions to our departments or divisions does not mean we are "overstepping our boundaries." In fact, nothing could be further from the truth! By taking responsibility for the goals of the company at large, we increase our visibility and showcase our leadership potential.

But don't just look around, look up! With your attention firmly focused on delivering your best performance in your current job—you should already be thinking, acting and speaking as if you were in the next job, at the next level of your career ladder.

Closing the culture gap

No matter where you are on your career journey—or where you're headed—your understanding of business culture will make the climb easier. In Chapter 1, I encouraged you to take a fresh look at your company by identifying sometimes subtle clues to its public image and private values. Keep up the detective work. This specialized knowledge can be your best guide to making career moves that are right for you—and speeding your professional progress.

Pass the popcorn

Your status as a business woman is up for review. Since the 1960s, the Women's Movement has boosted us into a strong position as independent thinkers and wage earners. With new trends afoot, our continued evolution during this decade demands that we become more proactive and anticipate rather than react to challenges. Faith Popcorn's very popular book, *The Popcorn Report*, can give you additional insight into developing trends and start you thinking about the role you'd like to play.

A personal game plan

In the first chapter, we stepped in close to evaluate the very individual "culture" of the company you work for—or plan to join. The purpose was to determine whether the "garden" you've chosen is conducive for you, as an individual, to grow and flourish professionally.

Now let's take the a step back. I invite you to take a *global* tour of your industry—or of several industries, if you wish—as you gather the following information. It may help guide you in a new and exciting career direction—or give you insights that will allow you to add value to your current employer—and strengthen your position.

1. Choose an industry

Are you working in the right industry? If you're not sure, you owe it to yourself to explore other industries. You may want to apply the skills of one industry—law, for example—to another, emerging industry, such as biotechnology or environmental planning.

Strategy: Don't just jump in! Spend some time at the library. Read industry publications and the business section of local and national newspapers. Talk to relatives, friends and *friends* of friends who work in your prospective industry or industries. Check out industry associations. Visit prospective companies. Will you need training or other credentials? Will you have to take a salary cut initially to make the jump?

It's important to take your time at this stage. Consider the time you spend as an investment in your future achievement. By making a concerted effort not to limit your scope, and then carefully examining all your options, you're already thinking like a leader.

2. Name the players

Once you've chosen your playing field—or industry—it's time to look at the players. Who are the industry leaders?

Strategy: The best way to analyze the detailed information you'll be gathering here is to create a "Chart of Competitors" showing a number of key categories, such as:

- Where is each company located? Are there branch offices or regional operations? How many?

- How—and how well—does each company differentiate itself from the rest of the field?

- What are the key similarities between one or more companies? Is there a gap no one seems to be filling?

- Are some players large, multi-product conglomerates? How well do they respond to the needs of the marketplace when pitted against smaller, more agile, single-product companies?

- What is the organizational structure? Public? Privately held? Are some of the companies part of a holding company?

- Who is the CEO of each company? What can you learn about their backgrounds, management styles and track records?

- Who are the other key players on the management team? What are their ages? How many women are represented? How did they get to that position?

- What efforts does each company make to listen to—and communicate with—its customers? If you can find customers to interview, ask them if they are satisfied. If not, what's missing?

- Ultimately, how does each company rank in market share? Is the number-one position solid or is there an innovative contender becoming a threat?

3. Look for success stories

What approaches have worked successfully for the companies? This is the time to be objective—especially if you already work for one of the contenders you're charting. Analyze current strategies used by each company. What works? How well? What new programs are on tap? How are they being tested and introduced to current and prospective customers?

Strategy: Get into the practice of questioning everything. If something isn't working—what might make it work? If something is working, how can it be improved? Don't fall into the trap of criticizing everything your competitors do out of loyalty for your current company—be objective! After all, they must be doing something right if they are perceived as any kind of threat to your hold on the market.

4. Identify a "winner."

Once you've examined their ways and means—is there a clear leader here? If you aren't working for the "winner," is there any idea, strategy or policy you could borrow and adapt for your own company?

Strategy: If you believe an idea has potential, keep it under your hat until you can "market test" its viability in informal conversations with your peers. If you still feel confident of its value, present it to your manager. Make sure your research is extensive enough to make a compelling argument for your plan, and proofread your written report or memo to make sure that your grammar, structure and logic are flawless.

Take care to package your idea in a way that makes your personal contribution clear. If you think there is a chance that your manager might try to repackage your idea as his/her own, cover your tracks with memos.

If—and only if—your organization's top management has an "open-door policy," take a deep breath and try out your presentation on the CEO. It's always wise to let your manager know what you're planning to do—and perhaps invite him or her to attend.

5. Interview your boss

Do you know your boss well? If not, it's time you got better acquainted. Your boss is an invaluable resource—often untapped to its full potential perhaps because of intimidation factors. But good communication with your boss can foster helpful mentoring and lead to better opportunities for you within the company—and even beyond.

Strategy: Ask your boss to lunch and ask for feedback on how well you're doing. Ask what specific skills you have that your boss feels are assets—and how you can build on them, and ultimately transfer them to the next level. Ask for insights, ideas and suggestions that may broaden your scope of understanding of your company and industry.

Don't forget to listen! By showing that you admire your boss's career achievements, you'll make a lasting impression. But you'll also be harvesting valuable information you can use as you progress.

6. Map your career path

Of course, you may find out that you and your boss have very different goals.

Strategy: On a sheet of paper, chart your boss' career path. What would you change to reach your own goals? Your aim is not to become a clone of your boss—simply to emulate his best qualities and learn as much as you can from his/her successes and mistakes. Your own individual talent and ideas will complete your career profile.

There is another potential byproduct of your interviews with your boss. You may discover you are being held back from opportunities you feel you should have, or that your boss sees your interest in your own growth as a threat to his or her position. Should you decide to look outside your department or company, your conversations with your boss should give you the poise and specific questions to better interview prospective new bosses.

Where to from here?

Onward and upward, I hope! Early in this century, it was customary to trust an employer to provide a career route—from first job to pension. In this self-contained world, hard work was supposed to pay off in promotion.

Loyalty was supposed to be rewarded with seniority and financial gain. We must stop depending on others for career direction and advancement!

These days, very few of us are waiting for that gold watch.

By taking your head out of the sand and taking a broad view of your world of work, you can move ahead more confident of who you are and where you're going. The opportunity is there. The rest is up to you.

4

Women at work: Greeting the revolution with open arms

Change. As human beings, we tend to shun it. If we could, most of us would stick to the tried-and-true—and probably still be in the Stone Age. So how did we get this far?

Look back and throughout history you'll see inevitable cycles of change. Certain events combined to create discomfort. Discomfort built to revolution. And when the dust settled—revolution left evolution.

At this juncture in history, we've witnessed some of the most dramatic events of this century. Political systems that had become entrenched as world powers suddenly toppled. A new economic structure is taking shape in Europe. Socially, we're waking up from the stupor of the "Me Generation" to find we're dissatisfied with the status quo in government and in business. In fact, many of us are beginning to see ourselves as members of a "global community"— ready to take greater responsibility for the care and well-being of each other and the planet.

Shaking it up

But not without plenty of stress. The process of evolution often tests us by firmly shaking our often unchallenged values, belief systems, customs and ways of life. As we work on finding a unified voice, there is bound to be chaos. If you're feeling overwhelmed and powerless, you're not alone. According to *Fortune* magazine, many of us are fighting back—to the tune of a record-breaking $300 billion in litigation against corporations annually!

While I don't promote reactionary acts such as this, I will tell you that now—with the tremors of change still shaking the ground under our feet—is the time for working women to begin reaching out for the many new opportunities uncovered. It's not likely to be easy. But if you take an active role in acquiring the necessary knowledge, skills and abilities, you can define an exciting and rewarding future. The fundamental shift in the world of work will press us to change some of our most basic attitudes—beginning with our beliefs about power.

Negotiating the "chain of command"

As we've seen, the organizational hierarchies fashioned by men during the Industrial Age reflected a military mentality. Gaining autocratic control and using it to keep employees "in line" was the goal. If there is a rigid hierarchy in place in your company, power may still be an absolute nonnegotiable force—directing even the most basic daily behavior, such as who can speak to whom.

So it's not surprising that power has gotten a bad reputation—especially with women. As a group, we tend to be uncomfortable with overt power. Some of us simply comply. Others have found subtle and clever ways to "work around it" to get what we want.

When I began my career after my children were in school, the power hierarchy in my company didn't make any sense to me. When I needed a quick answer, the old "chain of command" was just not expedient—or practical from a business perspective. After all, while I was working my way through multiple levels of hierarchy, the company could be losing ground with the competition!

Of course, I was always reprimanded for circumventing the rules. But I found that I could often deflect attention from my "subversive" acts by using humor. For example, when I passed over one "link" in the chain, I tried softening what might be perceived as a power play on my part by saying, "I hope I'm not stepping too far out on a limb to do my job...If I'm out of line, start sawing the limb!" Often, the executive would chuckle—and commend me for being thorough!

The many faces of power

What women need to learn is that power itself is not bad. Neither is it good. Like anything else, how it is used defines the way it is perceived. Here are some of the many faces of power you may already have seen:

Referent power. This power tends to be benign, because it is freely bestowed by others out of respect for personal attributes and achievements. People who are known as "natural leaders" have *referent power*.

Legitimate power. This is the power of authority and position. Your boss has *legitimate power* over you. If you are a manager, you have the same kind of power over the people who report to you.

Expert power. The specialized knowledge or information you have as an expert in your field—whether you're doctor, engineer or marketing guru—gives you power over the people who need it.

Reward power. Your ability to grant someone else something of material or personal value—such as a salary increase or promotion—gives you this benevolent power.

Coercive power. The flip side of the power to reward is the power to take away. If you can get others to do things using force—even if it is only the threat of action—you often have complete control. In business, *coercive power* can take the form of threatening dismissal or withholding privileges, status and salary increases. Like *reward power*, *coercive power* can be related to the *legitimate power* held by a boss. Unlike *reward power*, it tends to destroy—not foster—motivation when used unwisely.

Personal power. As women, we tend to soften the power we gain through position or achievement using interpersonal skills—such as influence. Instead of flaunting it, we can use *personal power* to build and nurture team spirit.

How many of these types of power do you recognize among the familiar faces you see everyday in your own company or business? What kinds of power do you have? What kinds would you like to acquire? Which type of power currently causes you the greatest concern? Which affirms you to become more than you currently are?

The danger of abusing power

Often the results of using power in a negative way are not readily apparent to the person or group wielding the power until communication and productivity are diminished.

"Layer cloning"

When power is tied to a specific role or level within a hierarchy, a company often inadvertently "clones" the members of each layer of management by prescribing strict standards for appearance and behavior. I've dubbed this organizational phenomenon "layer cloning."

Say, for example, you could line up the many vice presidents of a large organization, side by side. You'd probably be struck by the number of similarities they share—from the suits they wear to the language they use. By creating a small, uniform army of executives, the company can consolidate its power by reinforcing the values of the culture. This is the best way to kill dissenting viewpoints and create a "we-they" culture. But taken to its extreme, layer cloning promotes an insidious kind of stagnancy that can eat away at the energy and spirit of a company—from the inside out.

Means or end?

As a career counselor, I'm always astonished when young men and women tell me their career aspirations in a single statement: "I want to become a vice president." I can only smile and ask: "A vice president of what?" The answer is often a blank stare.

Early in my career, I thought this vice president fixation was a fluke. But after hearing it over and over, I've realized that, for some people, power and title is an end in itself. For this group, knowledge, skills and abilities are acquired only to gain more power.

The "Queen Bee"

What happens to some successful women who, after completing an arduous and impressive struggle to the top, become so consumed with the power they have achieved that they forget about everything that made them succeed?

Leona Helmsley probably best exemplifies the kind of self-made-woman-turned-power-monger. She made it to the top, only to horde power by breaking laws she clearly felt no longer applied to her. Instead of becoming invaluable role models to other women on the way up, Queen Bees are destructive to everyone, including themselves.

Women at the top: Cream or curdled milk?

Somewhere between the celebration and the continued reign, a devastating change occurs, heralded by signs that may be so subtle, they could escape observation. They tend to look like this:

- A concern to "micromanage," seeking to know all, see all and touch all that makes the business operate.

- A subtle fear of some unknown force that may dethrone or reduce power, often manifesting in a sense of distrust of those closest to her.

- Creating a "social spectacle" at community events where the Queen Bee needs to be the center of attention.

- Assigning demeaning activities to an inner circle of assistants, such as shopping for personal items, taking care of personal errands from car maintenance to housework.

- The development of disposable relationships; rather than nurturing the network that helped her reach her position, she destroys it.

- An arrogance that the Queen Bee knows all. She is rarely, if ever, to be questioned.

- Distancing herself from the rest of the company, perhaps cloistering herself in a penthouse-type environment.

This is indeed a sad reality that we've witnesses among a few women who've broken through the glass ceiling. While each female CEO I have known began with the purest of intents, some lost all levels of effectiveness and became the subject of community-wide ridicule for their flamboyance, arrogance and vanity. The net effect is that their reign of power, shorter than their male counterparts, became a joke and a negative role model for many women who saw the position discredited through the person who filled it.

My point is that with leadership comes responsibility and accountability. We must salvage the giftedness that earned us the throne in the first place. We must nurture it and not set it aside as we move into positions of power. We must not let the position mold us into a monolithic power monger like Leona Helmsley, who quickly upon getting her shopping list met, forgot all the little people. If we do so, we have prostituted ourselves, using others to get our reward, and then discarding the best of ourselves and the best that others brought to service.

Women, politics and the New Organization

In the Industrial Age, managers used fear to gain absolute control over a diverse group of employees. Fear may have gotten the desired reaction in the short-term—but there's no doubt that it destroyed long-term motivation. Gradually, we're realizing that we can enhance power by investing in relationships.

Count the professional relationships you develop throughout your career among your most precious assets. If you take care to actively nurture and maintain them by sharing information and offering support, they will bring unexpected rewards.

But burn even one bridge—by leaving a job without sufficient notice, for example—and you may be inviting unpleasant repercussions. The fact is, you never know when you may meet someone again. Many industries are notoriously incestuous. The co-worker you left high and dry today may become your boss somewhere down the road!

As women, we tend to be uncomfortable with friction or conflict at work. We prefer harmony. By contrast, men were raised to expect conflict as a natural part of even the friendliest business interactions. So, it makes sense that men may interpret our sensitivity as pettiness and inflexibility—and withhold promotion or leadership opportunities.

The lesson? Don't take differences at work personally! The sooner we can accept friction as a temporary cost of doing business, rather than a personal affront, the sooner we'll demonstrate to those in positions of authority that we have the attributes of leadership.

As girls, our first significant role models were our parents and teachers. Even then, we probably were as fascinated with the person as with the position. Meanwhile, men were raised to admire—and aggressively pursue—the power and prestige of position. Unfortunately, some have gone on to become gross caricatures of the arrogant boss—ruling through crisis management and always watching their backs.

These days, however, most of us realize the value of teamwork. But knowing how to create a cohesive team is another thing. One CEO used a sports analogy to describe his frustration at the lack of team spirit in his staff. "I arrive at work on Monday morning, suited up to play an aggressive game of football. My team assembles before me all wearing wet suits and snorkels!" he exclaimed. "I'm prepared to play a team sport, and they're all ready to solo into unsupervised waters...We are not even playing the same game!"

Although men may have more team experience from playing sports, most remain focused on competition. What we also need are *coaches* who look for ways to use the gifts of each player in order to ensure the success of the team. This is where our strengths as women can be a real asset.

As far back as 1971, studies showed that many women managers tended to create a unique type of power that integrated professional goals with personal relationships. The result was often a more effective working environment. If you're lucky enough to find this type of manager within your own organization, you've found a role model.

Are women helping other women?

Five years ago, my answer would have been an unequivocal "No!" But times are changing, slowly.

We've been intimidated by power brokers for too long. But in order to raise our professional profile and streamline our progress through the ranks, we need to actively court them. Like men, we need to work together to find creative ways to support each other.

Establishing a "clout" network

Traditionally, men have moved within an informal, interpersonal power structure known as the good old boy network. As women, we are excluded from this system. We don't speak the language or know the values—and most of us are sincerely baffled by the power of something that sounds so unassuming by name.

Clearly, it's time we had our own network. As we move from company to company and up within the ranks, all of us would benefit from working together to raise our profile as—dare I say it?—good old girls.

We're halfway there. The same skills you've used for years to develop professional contacts outside your organizations can be focused on creating powerful alliances that will help us all. By reaching out to offer encouragement, share information and find opportunities for the women who follow you through the ranks of business, you can enhance the image and stature of all women in the work force.

Resisting competition

I have a theory. I think that, as women, we may often resist helping one another because we still compete with each for the attention of males. With men still in positions of power in most companies, we are in the position of trying to impress men both personally and professionally.

This kind of thinking can set us all back 100 years! Sharing the attention of male managers with other professional women doesn't diminish your own worth. If you think you may be playing this dangerous game, make a searching inventory of your actions. Awareness is the first step to change.

It will take plenty of practice to begin thinking and acting differently. It's time to step out of the independent fortresses many of us have created for ourselves and team up with other capable women we admire.

What about discrimination?

We all know about the compensation gulf between men and women who perform the same job. But is there a similar gulf between women?

Unfortunately, it's all too common when women report to other women. I've counseled dozens of women during my career who are angry that their female bosses expect them to provide personal "maid service" as well as professional support!

Here's a case in point: One of two women reporting to a female CEO complained that she'd reached her limit when her boss asked her to help prepare for a lengthy international business trip by having her shop for a complete line of new underwear!

Her co-worker was equally disgruntled. She was left with the task of feeding the family's pet rabbit. Although neither of these women would think to complain about extra duties or overtime at the office, both felt their boss was being unreasonable. Surely, this CEO would never call on a man on her staff to buy her underwear. Why, then, would a woman who rose through the ranks herself be so insensitive toward the women who are following in her footsteps?

We'll talk more about role distortion that often occurs in women who hit the top later. Certainly it has a lot to do with the burden of being a "Superwoman" who can do it all—at work and at home.

More power in the workplace

Here's a strategy for enhancing your image and power right away.

1. Invest in relationships. There is no principle more fundamental and important. The more you can learn from others, the more you can give back by helping others. This skill is one we take for granted in the home and ignore in the organization. Who have you been overlooking? Remember to look outside of your department and cultivate people at different levels of your organization.

2. Establish credibility. Become more aware of your words and actions at work. Do you avoid conflict? Do you seem to give in too easily or show too much emotion in stressful situations? People are watching and making judgements about your leadership potential everyday. Work on meeting difficult situations head on with a positive, professional attitude.

3. Control information. Information is power. The more up-to-date you are on issues affecting your department and company, the greater your ability to exercise expert power. But don't believe everything you read—or hear. Ask plenty of questions.

4. Control resources. You'll enhance your professional credibility and leadership profile if you make every effort to be as careful with your budget at work as you are with your own money. Don't be stingy—but don't use your authority as *carte blanche* to overspend. Be clear about how you use limited resources, including equipment and staff positions. And always call attention to savings and extra value.

5. Tap hidden "pockets" of power. Don't rely exclusively on your organization chart, because every department or division has an informal leader who may have more real power than the defined leader. While most career experts advise against linking yourself socially with people at lower levels, it shouldn't surprise you that making an effort to be friendly and cooperative toward administrative staff members can turn them into invaluable professional resources.

6. Protect the power you have. Resist the urge to use coercive or other negative power. You may lose the power you have. Protect and build your power by being proactive. Look outside your own job and department to see how your actions and job affect others in the company. Working hard toward the goals that have been identified by your organization is the best revenge.

Obstacles and opportunity

I won't try to fool you. There are still many obstacles blocking your path to career success. Some are self-perpetuating, such as the Superwoman Syndrome and real or perceived sabotage from other professional women. These can be moved aside with awareness and effort. Others, such as sexual harassment, are slowly being exposed and will be harder to obliterate. To take advantage of the many new opportunities ahead, you'll have to develop skills to meet the needs of the present while actively anticipating the needs of the future. The good news is that you have strengths that you haven't begun to tap.

All you need to learn is how to play the game!

5

The New Organizational woman: Rediscovering your gifts

In examining history, structure and culture, we've been able to sketch a landscape of the world of business. But it is still only a background for the real activity—work. As a working woman, you are among the many main characters who bring it to life every day for 40 or more hours a week.

Do you feel at home? Have you learned to cultivate the many opportunities in your unique environment—or does it seem to resist your very best efforts?

How well you function as a woman in the workplace depends in large part upon how effective you are as an individual. While there are many things you can't control in your company or profession, the truth is that you can master many situations using your own skills and behavior. You can redirect your thoughts and attitude. You can learn more about your unique gifts, talents and personal qualities. Finally, you can become aware of the ways you may be limiting your own potential and begin to release yourself from your own restrictions.

It begins with the easiest thing to control—the way you look at the world around you.

It's all in the attitude

For most of us, "attitude" is a loaded word. If you've ever been accused of having a bad attitude, you may feel like you've been reprimanded for something so personal you couldn't possibly control it. The fact is that if you don't control your attitude, it can control and annihilate you.

Most of us have had to do something we thought would be impossible—only to pull it off. If your survival depends on the outcome, you'll find a way to ignore the "I think I can't" messages swirling around in your head.

But those messages are not so easy to ignore in situations you face every day. Where do they come from?

The media, family, friends and employers all provide you with constant input about yourself—your behavior, your appearance, your potential. It can range from the latest fashion magazine blitz of "perfect faces" to a single, disapproving glance. Along the way, you've collected plenty of inaccurate data about who you are and what you might be capable of achieving. The problem is that once you internalize "bad" data, you may work hard to support it through your behavior. The result? You create the outcome others expect!

Study after study has shown us the power of self-fulfilling prophecy. For example, if you tend to be shy, you may avoid social situations in which you'll encounter new people. Or you may become so self-conscious that you will *make* yourself fail. Even if you think you're focused on success, you may believe you'll only be capable of reaching a certain level—and excuse yourself from actions or commitment that might take you further!

Most of us don't live with the same reality. What you see is filtered through a system of beliefs you've adopted in the unique context of your own upbringing, culture, education and personal nature. To support your reality, you may be very selective about which events you remember. You probably ignore those that don't support your beliefs and gravitate toward people who have a similar view of the world.

Is your success a part of it? Not always. As women, we sometimes grow up with an unconscious fear of success. As little girls, we are taught to admire successful people for their talent and ambition. At the same time, we're assured that modesty and selflessness will bring us admiration. The confusing message is often clear only in hindsight: "Be successful. But don't act too aggressive!" In other words, too much success is not feminine.

Unlike many women, I can count my mother as a dominant force in my own success. Even today, she is my biggest cheerleader. But she also regularly sends these conflicting messages: "You're a workaholic" and "Do you only work to gain more possessions?"

Whenever I begin to tackle a new project, for a moment my natural enthusiasm and commitment is overshadowed by my mother's words. I don't blame her. She is expressing the ambivalence we've all experienced to some degree. The key to overcoming its influence is to recognize its hidden messages. Then gauge your response to your own goals, not external input or internal programming.

Dysfunction: From denial to crisis

In the past, companies have ignored the personal lives of workers. But that didn't stop many individuals from bringing their problems to work. Today, most New Organizations realize that employees who are grappling with personal issues and dysfunctional situations at work put a strain on other employees and overall productivity. Many offer plans to aid employees through counseling and other care.

If you have personal problems that threaten your productivity at work, remove these stumbling blocks. The following types of behavior are clues to personal and corporate dysfunction:

- Denial
- Confusion
- Self-centered behavior
- Perfectionism
- Dishonesty
- A focus on scarcity rather the abundance
- Controlling behavior
- A feeling of being "frozen" in action
- Unethical behavior

But what if the company itself is dysfunctional? An atmosphere of constant crisis is depressing for most individuals—and often leads even the healthiest to become dependent, defensive and blaming. If your instincts tell you this is happening in your environment, don't allow yourself to be consumed by it. Move on.

Programming yourself to succeed

The most imposing wall you may ever have to scale is built of your own self-defeating behaviors. As a career counselor, I have encouraged many women to begin to identify the faulty beliefs they have inherited or adopted over time—and then change their programming by changing their thoughts.

Am I asking you to be a Pollyanna? Not by a long shot. I'm simply challenging you to use your intelligence to view "reality" from a slightly different perspective. Use these steps as a guide.

The Smart Woman's Guide

1. Question your beliefs. This takes guts, so you should begin in complete privacy. Examine the beliefs you hold closest to your heart. Which do you value most? Which do you believe may be holding you back from what you want? Go with your first thoughts, and don't edit. This is an important part of the process of "tricking" yourself into looking at yourself objectively. Not an easy task! If it helps, begin by analyzing someone you know well. Or pretend you are another person. It will be easier to be objective.

2. Isolate those self-fulfilling prophecies. As a woman, you should be especially vigilant to self-fulfilling behaviors you may have developed in response to a constant barrage of messages from the media. Fashion magazines, television and advertising often set impossible standards for physical beauty and age. If you've bought into any of these standards and fall short of them (and we all do, to a greater or lesser degree)—check your self-esteem!

If you weigh a few pounds more than the latest supermodel, do you feel others won't be interested in what you have to say at work? Or do you put your professional goals on hold until you lose the weight? Ridiculous, isn't it?

3. Talk back. Now write a statement that transforms each self-fulfilling behavior into its opposite. For example, "Although I may be a few pounds over the media ideal, I'm completely comfortable with the way I look." Get positive support from family and friends. Write down their words and read them each day, to reinforce your new internal tapes.

What if you decide you could lose a few pounds? It's OK to write, "I'm working on it." After all, everyone should have a number of goals, professional and personal, in the works. Just be sure you're doing what is important to you.

I advise you to begin treating your thoughts as visitors, not masters. If they are friendly and supportive, ask them back. If not, feel no shame in banishing them! At first, it will be difficult to push them aside. You've invested a lot in supporting them over the years. Other self-defeating thoughts may rush in to fill the gap. But keep pushing away the self-defeating thoughts and replacing them with positive and powerful self-fulfilling prophecies. It's a bit like brainwashing yourself. But I promise you that soon you'll notice you really are thinking differently.

4. Create a new reality. Now, you're going to come out in the open with your *new* behavior. It won't be easy—at first. So take small steps. Create situations that are likely to support your new behavior with immediate and obvious results. With each success, you can take a bigger stride.

If, for example, you're terrified of making presentations, begin practicing in front of a mirror. Then try a short speech out on your family or co-workers. It does get easier. That's good to know, since you should expect to be improving your reality throughout your lifetime! With practice, you'll recognize a self-defeating thought at 20 yards, and simply turn your back.

Who are you—really?

If you're tempted to reel off your roles—mother, sister, friend, student, professional—or your education and professional credentials, go ahead and get it out of your system. Now, what makes you unique—unlike anyone else in your family or company? In counseling women over the course of my career, I've found few who have a clear idea. If this is virgin territory, enter with joy, not trepidation.

We all have very special gifts—talents, abilities and personal qualities that come easy to us. If you don't recognize them, you can't capitalize on them. This 20 percent of your professional assets is your advantage—like a golfer's handicap. It can take you 80 percent of the way toward our goals. The other 20 percent of the way will require all the knowledge and perspiration you can muster.

If you need help zeroing in on your "20-percent asset," complete the following inventory, borrowed from Naomi Stephan's *Finding Your Life Mission*. Check the attributes in each of the four lists below that you feel best match your behavior and personal qualities. Be honest, but don't take too much time to think. That's what so often trips us up! After you total the marks under each column, read a description of your personality type on the following pages.

Doer

❏ Bold
❏ Strong-willed
❏ Decisive
❏ Competitive
❏ Self-assured
❏ Tension-producer
❏ Pragmatic
❏ Blunt
❏ Tough
❏ Impatient
❏ Dominating
❏ Cold
❏ Action-oriented
❏ Self-starter
❏ Accepts challenge
❏ Likes risks
❏ Forceful opinions
❏ Disciplined, quick
❏ Works on hunches
❏ Accepts challenges

Total: _____

Motivator

❏ Generous
❏ Enthusiastic
❏ Influential
❏ Gullible
❏ Humorous
❏ Imaginative
❏ Charming
❏ Emotional
❏ Self-promoting
❏ Impulsive
❏ Manipulative
❏ Dramatic
❏ Trusts a lot
❏ High contact person
❏ Uses intuition
❏ Likes persuasion
❏ Likes fun jobs
❏ Likes to motivate
❏ Dislikes details
❏ Visionary

Total: _____

Stabilizer

- ❑ Understanding
- ❑ Responsive
- ❑ Agreeable
- ❑ Calm
- ❑ Supportive
- ❑ Dependable
- ❑ Traditional
- ❑ Low-key
- ❑ Team player
- ❑ Predictable
- ❑ Loyal
- ❑ Thorough
- ❑ Good listener
- ❑ Logical
- ❑ Sticks to procedure
- ❑ Works in small groups
- ❑ Likes structure
- ❑ Quiet in meetings
- ❑ Methodical
- ❑ Traditional

Total: _____

Analyzer

- ❑ Conventional
- ❑ Organized
- ❑ Orderly
- ❑ Unresponsive
- ❑ Indecisive
- ❑ Exacting
- ❑ Orderly
- ❑ Restrained
- ❑ Critical
- ❑ Disciplined
- ❑ Meticulous
- ❑ Proper
- ❑ Evaluates
- ❑ Works alone
- ❑ Slow-paced
- ❑ Non-verbal
- ❑ Business-like
- ❑ Respects facts
- ❑ Problem-solver
- ❑ Likes clarity

Total: _____

What's your type?

If there is a clear majority from one column, you know who you are. But many times, the totals for two columns will be close. This shows you have integrated the qualities of two different personality types. See how unique you are? Read the descriptions below for detail.

Doers

If you're a doer, you are driven to produce results. You often tend to dominate groups—in fact you're likely to be in charge. You're probably more serious than anyone—except another Doer—about staying focused and quickly completing the task at hand.

You're motivated by: Achievement and competition. You're in your element when you can call the shots from a position of power.

You often appear to be: Aloof and lacking in emotion when you're in the throes of work. Professionally and personally, you always have a mission in the works.

You dislike: Wasting time. Because you often test yourself by compressing deadlines, you can become impatient with others (and yourself) when you fall behind schedule for any reason.

Motivators

If you're a motivator, you're passionate about having fun. You use your spontaneity to involve other people. You value relationships and are responsive to the needs and contributions of many types of individuals.

You're motivated by: Recognition. You love the challenge of persuading others to buy your ideas and products.

Your often appear to be: Outgoing, optimistic, a real "people person." You thrive on "performing" in the social arena. Yet, you often go out of your way to demonstrate affection and concern for others.

You dislike: Anybody who feels "vanilla" about anything!

Stabilizers

If you're a stabilizer, you're the "glue" that holds a team together. Cautious and conservative by nature, you are dependable—and tend to be a loyal, long-time employee.

You're motivated by: Quality. You like to take your time to produce quality work. You may prefer cyclical or repetitive tasks because you like to be able to budget your time and energies.

You often appear to be: Good natured, unhurried and amiable. You are known for investing in long-term relationships.

You dislike: Surprises. You prefer advance notice of changes that will require contingency plans. You're in your element when you can be proactive, rather than reactive.

Analyzers

If you're an analyzer, you value precision. You are the documentation, detail-driven member of any team.

You're motivated by: Accuracy. More than any other member of the team, you are concerned about the consequences of your actions. So, you prefer to work with data and analysis—often more than with other people.

You often appear to be: A perfectionist. You tend to be meticulous about organization and invest in structured working boundaries.

You dislike: Snap decisions. You'd rather wade through reams of data than make a decision that you won't be able to defend over time.

Putting it all together

By making this type of an assessment of your personality and gifts, you'll be better prepared to put them to work in the right environment, job and career.

For example, say you're a Motivator. As someone who thrives on the attention and company of a lot of other people, it doesn't make much sense to seek out a solitary technical position inside a computer company. You would do better in sales.

But don't panic and make a quick career change! Take some time to think about how you could change your present job to suit your personality. If not, you may be able to make a lateral move within your present organization to become an customer service representative, for example.

Find the right job. Just don't ignore your personality in the pursuit of money or prestige. You'll only work harder to succeed. The more we try to fit a square peg into a round hole, the greater the stress on the peg. Conversely, doing what you love and can naturally do well often seems effortless.

Do what you love, and you're bound to feel stimulated and invigorated because you're interested and challenged. In my experience, the women who love what they do are often the happiest and most fulfilled professionals I know. Because they are personally as well as professionally motivated, they contribute more. Their contributions make them stand out and they tend to be promoted faster than women—or men, for that matter—who aren't having so much fun!

The power of presence

Your personality—all the things about you that make you unique from anyone else—can give you real presence as a professional. In full flower, personality is the self-assurance that comes through self-control. When you recognize and value your individual strengths, you have the determination to banish any "faulty" attitudes and beliefs that diminish your potential. Without personality, you are nothing more than a cardboard executive—cold and wary of standing out from the crowd.

So, celebrate your unique gifts. They can be the key to your success.

6

Overcoming personal and professional roadblocks

Let's face it. Even if you have the most positive attitude, it's a jungle out there! As a businesswoman, you are an explorer in terrain that can be fraught with professional and personal obstacles. But I'd wager you're also an adventurer with the courage and cunning to make it through.

If you were going into a real jungle, you'd want to know everything you could about the geography and climate. Are the natives friendly? What predators might be lurking out there? How will you dodge poison arrows? How do you keep your cool and keep making progress in the right direction?

You don't have to be Stanley or Livingston. But it would help to have a "map" to negotiate obstacles in the business world—even its deepest and darkest, such as sexual harassment. You'll also need information on where you're likely to find such obstacles and their degree of difficulty.

First things first. When you set up the camp you'll use as home base for your explorations, you want to make sure it is in the right place.

Organizational obstacles: The environment

In many ways, a company is like a club. If you champion its values and follow its bylaws, you're a member in good standing. You may be rewarded with an office or asked to chair an event. If you don't have the same values—and you're not asked to leave—you may become a *persona non grata*.

Because a company's values determine what decisions are made, how problems are solved, how and when people are rewarded, even the benefits extended to employees, it's important to recognize the kind of club you've joined. Is it the right club for you?

Six basic value systems

According to a model developed by William Spranger, people tend to be motivated by one or more of six basic types of value systems. I've found the same value systems drive most of the businesses I've worked with. As you review the value systems here, don't be surprised if you find that more than one is at work in your company. It may take close examination to determine which is the dominant system.

1. Theoretical. Innovation is valued in this environment. In fact, ideas may be the only products produced. To this end, think tanks, universities and other research-oriented businesses turn employees loose with all the time and resources they need to create and develop new concepts and abstract models that will enlighten us—or might change the world.

This is a serious, often subdued atmosphere—filled with books, computers, flip charts with scribbled formulas and creative models of work in progress.

2. Economic. A world away are the companies driven by the almighty dollar. No matter what the product, the focus is on the bottom line. If you're a member of this club, you must understand that you will always come second to profit. To get ahead, you value practicality and discard anything that doesn't involve a payback—even if your decisions conflict with human issues. You will continually be challenged to demonstrate return on investment.

3. Aesthetic. Creative energy infuses the products and working environment of businesses such as advertising agencies. Here, individual talents are revered and aesthetic harmony is encouraged. A dramatic decor is often a visual reflection of this process—underlining a commitment to producing a quality product that has distinctive visual appeal.

4. Social. Hospitals or environmental organizations share a dedication for the kinds of humanitarian causes that drive this type of business. Whatever the cause, it clearly takes precedence to the professional trappings that are important to many other businesses. People are important. But to get ahead, you will have to be passionate about your work—even if the pay is low and perks are minimal.

5. Political. Whether they're after influence or market dominance, these companies value power. To get head, you'll have to be driven to acquire it and committed to showing it off. In this environment, there are often as many power struggles going on among members as there are with outside competitors.

6. Regulatory. Standards keep these companies on the straight and narrow. Your only route to effectiveness is by way of a detailed, systematic approach—using legislative, regulatory or other standard operating procedures. As a member, your commitment to consistency and accuracy will bring you success.

Align your values with the organization

Now that you've identified the value system that drives your company, how well do you think *your* values fit? If you are motivated by the aesthetic system of values and you're slaving away in an *economic* environment, you probably already feel the strain. If you own your own design studio, you may feel the tug of many value systems in running your business and serving clients—from economic to political.

The more closely aligned your values are with the values of your company or business organization, the more comfortable you'll feel going to work every day—and the more successful you'll be over the long term.Often "non-fits" become apparent in your gut before the message travels to your head.

What if you need to find a better fit? If you've joined the *wrong* club, can you change your values? Not very easily. By the time we become adults, most of us have formed a strong personal value system which is often non-negotiable. Similarly, the values of your business or company may be inextricably bound up with an industry or tradition of leadership. It's probably best to begin scouting around for a company that shares your values.

Working within the value system

If you find your value system is in sync with your company's values, here's a step-by-step plan that will help you maximize your contributions as a member:

1. Look for successful people. The people who have already achieved success—whether through status, position or accomplishment—should be your role models. What paths did they take? What values did they bring to the company? How have they been rewarded? How do they contribute to perpetuating the company's value system?

2. Develop associations. If you can, establish a professional relationship with at least one of these "success stories." Ask each person how he or she works within your company's value system. What are some of the important lessons they learned in the process? Look for value statements in company literature and match them against the actions of successful people within the company. How do your company's values differ from those of competing companies?

3. Avoid losers. Every company has at least one "professional victim"—an individual who would rather complain about his or her lack of recognition within the company than work harder or look for a more suitable environment. Watch out! This person's insecurity about his or her own lack of success may prompt hostile acts, such as sabotage. It is important to realize that losers need attention and to give it to them promotes their victimization. To get close to such a person will encourage others to view *you* in the same light—guilt by association.

4. Give—and receive. It's important to consistently share information and resources with your professional peers. But it's just as important to be able to receive information—whether in the form of a compliment or feedback. Many people are not comfortable accepting a compliment. What a shame! The next time you get ready to brush off someone else's genuine praise, stop. Take a moment to acknowledge the compliment and publicly thank the person who offered it. Then take a private moment to pat yourself on the back. Someone else noticed your efforts. Good job!

By the same token, it's important to be open to other kinds of feedback—even criticism. Resist the urge to disregard feedback from others until you've taken the time to evaluate it in light of the credentials and motives of the person who offers it. If you receive feedback that could improve your performance, take notice! Be appreciative and learn from the input.

5. Have many "baskets." You know the adage about putting all your eggs in one basket. It's also true, that these days you can no longer afford to pour all your career aspirations into one opportunity. Consider many options. Cultivate many possibilities. You can never predict how things will change in the years ahead. So, it's wise to protect yourself and make the most of your many assets.

Obstacles of gender: Discrimination

Yes, Virginia, discrimination continues to exist in almost every area of business. But that doesn't mean we have to be its victims. As women, we've made significant inroads over the years by simply working harder to succeed.

Are we perpetuating the problem? We may be. Many women still tend to defer to men in a business setting. We may be less likely to speak up or too quick to acquiesce. According to Toni Bernay, a psychologist and co-author of the book *Women in Power: The Secrets of Leadership*, "Timidity does us in more than aggression, because we become invisible."

Many of us already put in more time and more energy than our male counterparts to do the same jobs. Is this fair? Of course not. But it is working. We are slowly and steadily proving we can do the job. As we gain confidence in our abilities and accomplishments, it will be easier to speak up—and firmly and dispassionately request the rewards to which we are entitled.

Our focus should be on creating solutions—beginning on the personal level. Plan for situations you're likely to face in the future. What will you say? How should you act in order to diffuse discrimination? You should draw on every shred of information and experience available to you when dealing with different types of people, operating within the culture of your company.

Discrimination is a very emotional issue. But, it's important to remember that business is not focused on discrimination. It is focused on producing profit. Our best professional efforts are our best "weapon" against the discrimination that keeps us from contributing the coffers.

Taking on sexual harassment

October 1, 1991. As the world watched, Anita Hill, a young black professor from the University of Oklahoma, went before a Senate Committee to publicly oppose the nomination of her former boss, Clarence Thomas, as a Supreme Court Justice on the grounds of sexual harassment.

Using the media as a forum for "exploring" this loaded issue has its drawbacks. Many people saw the Hill-Thomas hearings as an embarrassing fiasco. Yet, it gave all of us who watched a clear idea of the gap in male awareness of sexual harassment in the workplace. By shining a spotlight on this controversial issue, the Hill-Thomas hearings flung open the door for other working women facing similar situations to speak out. As a result, many companies have developed explicit, printed policies for dealing with sexual harassment.

Much ado about "honey"

Fall, 1992. After a distinguished 25-year career, Dr. Frances K. Conley announced her resignation from Stanford University Medical School. The professor of nuerosurgery claimed discrimination blocked her opportunities for advancement and publicly objected to the behavior of many of her male colleagues. According to Dr. Conley, male professors regularly used *Playboy* centerfolds in lectures, referred to her as "honey" and made references to PMS whenever she disagreed with them.

But Dr. Conley focused the bulk of blame on one man—the acting chairman of the department—who validated this behavior by practicing it himself.

Working around the "male ego"

No doubt there will be more stories that are brought to national attention in the years ahead. But how do you handle personal situations you encounter every day? Often, tact and understanding prove to be powerful antidotes.

Who among us is a stranger to the "male ego"? We've been working around it in our personal relationships for years. So why not try transferring those "skills" to the work place?

Personal obstacles: Get out of your own way

Comedian Jack Parr said it well, "My life seems like one long obstacle course, with me as the chief obstacle." Most of the personal obstacles we face are of our own making. If you can understand why and how you trip yourself up in certain situations, you can begin to get out of your own way.

Facing fear

Fear can immobilize women faster than anything I know. It can shut down the confidence you have worked so hard to cultivate. What makes us so afraid? Our aspirations seem to be coupled with fears that can suffocate them: thinking about the goal automatically invites the fear.

Strategies: Fear is a powerful bugaboo. But like the monster under the bed, you can banish it by using a few simple techniques. Talk to yourself. If you hear a voice that says, "But, I won't be able to do it!" in your head, answer it with an adamant "Yes, I will!" Say it out loud, if you're alone! Then proceed to outline why and how you will accomplish what you know you can do.

Here's another technique: Write down every fear that blocks you on paper to acknowledge it. Then crumple up the paper and throw away the fear.

Finding direction

I once spoke to a mother of three about her career aspirations. She told me that she no longer wanted to be a medical technician, but she didn't have any idea what she wanted to be. Over the next three years, we had the same conversation several times. At the end of that time, she still didn't know where she was going. As a a result, all roads lead there.

Strategies: To locate other areas that spark an interest for you, get lots of information. Your local business library can be a rich resource. Read industry publications. Conduct "information interviews" with people working in industries and jobs you might want to pursue. Take an introductory course in another field. Even if you have no idea where you'll end up, you must make an effort to take the first steps yourself. Your interests will guide you the rest of the way.

Blowing your own horn

As women, we tend to be shy about promoting ourselves. Unlike our male colleagues, we weren't encouraged to brag or blow our own horns about our successes. Instead, we tend to understate our achievements and elevate others and their achievements at the expense of your own self-esteem.

Strategy: Make a list of power words to describe your skills and accomplishments. Then describe the value of your efforts and past accomplishments using concrete data—such as market share, time saved, profit. Quantify everything you can. This is a good business exercise (one that you should be doing regularly). And you are likely to be astounded by the impact you have in your job. When you've recovered, talk about it—using your concrete data.

Celebrating every victory

Unfortunately, women are notorious for not supporting one another. Ask a man! This behavior is shortsighted and holds all of us back. Instead of ignoring or thwarting each other's progress, we should be celebrating every victory made by women. The compound effect will help us all.

Strategy: Join a management organization that actively speaks to and promotes the efforts of professional women. If you can, interest other women in your division or company in joining, and talk informally about what you're learning. Cultivate an internal network of professional women and share information and resources. Actively spread the good word about the women who have succeeded. Regularly encourage other women who show promise as they continue on the way. Let your own efforts be an inspiration to others.

When you make a mistake: A strategy

You can expect to make mistakes during your career. Some will be minor and can be easily overlooked. But there may come a time or two when the results are humiliating. A friend might forgive and forget. Your company is not likely to. What to do? First, remind yourself that it is not the end of the world. Then:

1. Handle yourself with aplomb. We will be judged less for the mistake itself than how we handle it once it is made. It's hard to think clearly at times like these, so it is essential to be objective about the repercussions. If your assistant made the same mistake, how would you expect him or her to behave? What would it take to rectify the situation?

As women, we tend to beat ourselves up whenever we make a mistake. But resist the urge to retreat into yourself. You'll only invite more attention and criticism.

2. Remove yourself from the "scene of the crime." Don't react immediately. Find a private place, if you can, and spend a few moments breathing deeply to regain your composure. Then, think about the consequences and evaluate the outcome of each approach you might try.

3. Acknowledge the mistake. Clearly and dispassionately, go back over the details of what happened—and how it happened—with your boss. Let him or her know that you realize the consequences of what you've done—even if the worst didn't occur.

4. Explain what you plan to do about it. Don't leave out this important step. Simply acknowledging the mistake may get you a sympathetic hearing, but your boss will be interested in knowing that you learned something from your error and are not likely to repeat it.

At home in the jungle

There will always be obstacles. But the jungle is really not such a scary place. If you focus less on the limitations in the work place—and in yourself—you can concentrate on your own performance, you can cover a lot of ground.

7

Office relationships: Making the team

It's Monday morning and the men in your department gather to replay the weekend's sport events. Boys will be boys, right? Don't dismiss this ritual so lightly! There's something more going on here than sports fans trading game scores and player statistics. These Monday-morning quarterbacks are tossing around terminology that can give you deeper insight into the world of business.

Even if you don't follow sports, you're probably familiar with "sports-speak." (After all, you're not "out in left field.") To most women, these buzzwords make general sense. But one word can speak volumes in exchanges between men who understand its full meaning in the context of the sport.

For example when someone suggests you "huddle," what should you expect to accomplish? If you're asked to "punt"? Not sure? Read on.

Business as usual

The business world has borrowed terms from a number of popular professional sports to describe every position on your department's "team," as well as duties, responsibilities and territorial limitations. Even the verbs are used to inspire and motivate you to, say, "tackle" the job.

Depending on the favorite sport of the man in charge, sports vocabulary can differ from department to department within your company. Your department's sport of choice may even provide clues to its values. For example, baseball has a more leisurely pace than the hard-driving, high-scoring game of basketball. Football is all about strategy and the art of deception. In fact, if you're working with a group of football fanatics, you may be in the company of a future management team.

Jock or team player?

Does this mean you should bone up on football so you can join the huddle on Monday? Not necessarily. What you should do is learn the meaning of the terms, so you can use them to translate what's going on around you. So you don't "fumble."

If your boss tells you your job is "essentially to run interference," what does he expect from you? First you must understand that the football player who runs interference is assigned to clear a path through other players on the field to make it easier for the quarterback to carry the ball toward the goalpost and score. Then, you'll know you should be doing everything you can to ease your boss' workload—including anticipating the moves of other company players who still might try to block his efforts—so that he can concentrate on carrying out the department's goals. Most importantly, you're clear that you shouldn't pick up the ball and run with it yourself! Sound silly? It's very neat and efficient, once you get the hang of it. And it often helps ever-competitive men save face with each other.

For example, a manager may tell his subordinate, "I like to think I'm the quarterback" when presented with an opposing viewpoint. If the subordinate knows football, he'll understand his boss to mean, "You've argued enough for your viewpoint. It's time to drop it. I've already made the decision." But many women are not familiar with the role of a quarterback. You might return a blank stare—or make the mistake of continuing to argue your point!

Suiting up to play

It's time for women to get off the sidelines and into the game. The best way to score more points is to understand the rules. Here's a brief glossary of common sports terms used in business settings. For a more detailed guide to the nuances of the sports ethic within many companies, I recommend the still current classic, *Games Mother Never Taught You, Corporate Gamesmanship for Women* by Betty Lehan Harragan.

Baseball

Ball-park (figure). A rough dollar estimate, often used to determine whether further negotiation is warranted.

Out in left field. So far out of the action that you don't know what's going on. You may even be excluded from important inside information.

Team player. Someone who subordinates his or her efforts for the good of the team, or to allow the boss to take the credit.

Football

Huddle. To meet with co-workers in order to devise a plan for getting your point across to beat the competition. You might also "huddle" to make a deal that is beneficial for all the players.

Jock. A thoroughly competitive player. Not a "team player," but a professional who is serious about playing hard to win.

Monday-morning quarterback. Someone who delights in explaining "how it should have been done" or "how I would have done it"—after the fact.

Punt. To gamble on gaining points in what appears to be a no-win situation by making a desperate move, often kicking the ball.

Quarterback. The key player who "manages" the plays by telling other football players what to do in the huddle.

Tackle (the job). To approach a task with single-minded concentration.

What team are you on?

No matter what sports team you're on, once you get out there on the playing field, the name of the game is competing to win. Some teams have offensive strategies. Some are organized around the moves of a star quarterback. Some companies seem to promote frequent "skirmishes" between internal teams, rather than focusing on beating the outside competition.

Understanding the dynamics of the male sports ethic doesn't mean you'll win every time. Every season of your career will tell a different story. But as your needs change and your skills improve, your professional relationships with an array of team members can carry you through.

The rules of relationships

Most of us have two agendas at work. We need to gather the information and resources to complete the task or project at hand. But we also need help with personal issues, such as developing business maturity and coping with change. In every professional relationship there is the opportunity for the exchange—of information and support—that will benefit both sides.

All relationships depend on exchange. In a successful two-way relationship, information is always flowing back and forth. If you give your boss support that will make him or her "look good" in the company, you may expect recognition, greater challenge, more money, more exposure or all of the above.

All relationships change. It is naive to believe that they won't. Every one of us grows and changes over time, so it's only logical that our needs will also change. Some relationships may serve a purpose for a brief period during your career. Others will continue on—even if they're not active in every phase. Cherish both kinds.

Look at your current professional relationships. How have they changed over time? Have you been successful in redefining your exchanges, or have they simply evolved? Try to anticipate how each one may change within the next year. How will you handle it? Maintaining open communication is still the best way to protect a good relationship. But it takes two, so don't expect every relationship to evolve smoothly. Some relationships seem to have a built-in degree of difficulty, such as relationships between superiors and their subordinates.

Superiors and subordinates

Power is an underlying or overt force in this relationship. How much control does the boss want? As a young and ambitious new hire, you may seek career guidance and support over power. If you've accumulated some experience and accomplishments, you may pose a threat to your boss by seeking the same kind of support.

Traditionally, men have been "superiors" in working relationships. As our work force becomes more diverse, we face other equally, if not more, challenging types of relationships—such as women managing men and women managing women. Despite the diverse individuals involved, too many superior/subordinate relationships continue to fail because both people lack realistic expectations of what they can provide to—and expect from—each other.

Take responsibility for making this important relationship strong and productive early on. In an informal meeting or review, let your boss know what is important to you, what you expect to learn and achieve in your job. Then make sure you clearly understand what kind of contribution the boss expects from you. As these needs change or as a regular part of every performance review, update your "mutual expectations" agenda.

The older employee

As a young manager, how do you handle the resentment of an older woman working for you? I've found through experience, that women who work for younger women often feel threatened. They may feel they'll lose job security or lose out when it comes to growth or salary rewards. On closer examination, this is less an issue of age than of personal differences that could be easily answered through communication.

If you manage an older woman who is valuable to your department, make a special point to reassure her about the importance of her contributions to the department—and the company. Praise her for past accomplishments. Tell her you rely on her experience. Get her to talk about her goals and her worries about her future "chances" within the company.

Once things are out on the table, you can diffuse anger or feelings of frustration. If you follow through with support and encouragement according to the unique needs she has expressed, you are likely to have a valuable professional asset—and champion for life.

When men report to women

What was once a business anomaly is now common in most companies. In fact, young men entering the work force may expect to work for a woman just as often as for a man. Again, it all comes down to keeping the lines of communication open. Don't assume that everything is fine because you don't hear any differently.

I made that mistake. When I hired a young man to manage one of my groups, I couldn't have been more pleased. He was bright, gifted and had a stellar professional reputation. It wasn't long before he became known as a superior consultant within the company.

Although the company valued propriety and hierarchy, I accepted his "laid-back" style and nontraditional work habits. For example, in a presentation to the executive team, he joked, "If I had known that I would be facing such an esteemed group, I would have worn clean socks!" He clearly meant his remark to be an icebreaker. But the stunned look on the female CEO's face said it all, and he never regained the ground he once had.

Soon, I began to hear subtle comments that he "lacked the appropriate decorum" to become my successor. Although I defended him rigorously, I was surprised to hear him say, nearly a year after his hire, "I've come to the conclusion that I don't like working for a female..."

Now, I always ask male candidates whether they have ever reported to a woman. If their answer is yes, we can discuss their experiences as well as how my management style might differ. I find that, by giving them permission to be open about previous problems as well as current concerns, I can uncover any grievances or inhibitions that might cause problems in the future.

A professional relationship assessment

Here is a plan for evaluating your relationship with your current boss. As you answer each of the following questions, make note of any areas that could use some improvement.

1. What resources can your boss provide? At this stage of your career what do you need the most? Guidance—through plenty of feedback about your work and frank advice about areas of improvement? Introductions to other professionals in your company or industry who might help your career? More challenging work—with a "net"—so you can safely stretch your abilities?

2. What resources can you provide to your boss? Generally, the more successful your boss is, the more successful you will be. Can you take on additional tasks? Or suggest new policies—such as methods for marketing your department's efforts internally? What information do you pick up in conversations with your peers in other departments that might be useful to your boss? Does your boss depend on you to model positive behavior for other staff members? The important thing is to be honest about your ambitions and goals.

3. Which needs appear to be complementary? If the boss is planning to move on, he or she may be looking for someone to groom for the role. Does this fit into your plans? Your boss might need a trusted ambassador to represent him or her at trade shows and management meetings. Could your career use a shot of visibility?

4. Which needs conflict? Why? If your boss feels you are too ambitious—that your full attention and commitment are not on the immediate tasks—he or she may try to limit your growth. If you're looking for guidance and feedback, is your boss accessible?

5. How will you meet the needs not met by your boss? Cast your net wide to include professional organizations, contacts in your company, professional courses or an advanced degree. Document each contribution you make in memos so you can present the results of your work when you move on. If you feel you must move on soon, quietly begin to groom someone else to step into your place so that you can maintain a good professional relationship with your boss after you leave.

The mentor: The professional parent

It's been happening informally for some time. An established professional takes a protégé under wing—often nurturing and guiding the younger person to follow in his or her own footsteps. But not everyone is fortunate enough to find a willing mentor.

Formal mentoring programs are becoming more common in large organizations, as a means of accelerating the learning curve so that new employees can be more productive earlier in the game. Those that work, work exceedingly well. People who are the products of successful mentor relationships often fit in more quickly, earn higher salaries and tend to be happier with their jobs and the progress of their careers.

If the "match" is not right or if sexual innuendo or sexual harassment enter in, however, mentoring relationships can be damaging to fledgling professionals.

It's not necessary for your mentor to also be your boss. In fact, it may be more helpful to find someone elsewhere in the company or your industry who has confidence in your ability and is willing to promote you and your accomplishments in casual conversations with his or her peers.

From a vantage point of age and experience—and often executive position with the company—a mentor can help you understand the "big picture" as a context for your current work. When painful lessons must be learned, your mentor can reinforce the lesson in a way that is consoling rather than punishing. Generally, the more powerful your mentor is, the clearer your path to promotion is likely to be.

When it's time to leave

Just as there are signs that clearly indicate to you that you may need a mentor, there are also signs that will tell you it is time to leave the relationship. For example:

- **The relationship plateaus.** You may find very little or no new advice or counsel coming from your mentor.

- **You leave the organization.** If your mentor was prominent in your company, the context of the relationship will change when you leave. You may be able to maintain it from within another company. If not, make sure it lasts as a professional friendship.

- **Your attitude changes.** Your mentor may become cynical or you may find yourself forcing enthusiasm during your time together. These negative feelings will only continue to build, so it's wise to reestablish your relationship—as professional colleagues.

- **You're not being challenged.** As you mature, many of your initial hesitancies will melt away. If you're comfortable and confident testing your wings, you may find it's time to fly solo. Don't feel badly about this time. Leaving the nest is the ultimate goal of this type of relationship—a legitimate and necessary rite of passage in the business world.

Your peers: The value of mutual support

Because you're not responsible for evaluating each other's performance, the pressure is off in a relationship with a co-worker. Now you can begin to support each other's efforts and gain valuable practice working together to solve real problems. The sad reality is that competition within a company often prevents individuals from really benefiting from peer relationships. You can win by initiating collaborative efforts—especially in a competitive environment.

While networking within your company is a skill I encourage, it also pays to broaden your perspective. Join organizations. Talk to people working in your position within another company to gain a broader frame of reference for your career. Aside from gaining valuable contacts you may be able to draw on in the future, you'll be gaining influence within a wide circle of professionals Remember, it is a critical ingredient to career success to broaden and deepen your circle of influence!

Laughing it off

The strongest relationships often depend on humor. Laughing regularly can diffuse anger and stress and improve your creativity and effectiveness. A good sense of humor makes good sense. How does yours measure up?

1. What do you laugh at? Are you always making fun of yourself? It's OK to indulge in a good-natured laugh at your mistakes, but don't use humor at your own expense—or anyone else's.

Forget ethnic or tasteless jokes. Stick to puns and clever wordplay. Even good-natured teasing.

2. How do you laugh? Do you giggle? Chuckle? Laugh loudly? Do you repress laughter so that others won't see? If you're working in a somber environment, it may be inappropriate to laugh. When you find yourself holding back your humor, it may be time to look for a more lighthearted group.

3. How often do you laugh? Has it been too long? How can you infuse some merriment into your group?

4. How often do you smile during a regular business day? Do you smile when you answer the phone so that your voice sounds welcoming and supporting?

5. Why do you smile? Many women smile too often—and laugh at inappropriate times, to take the "sting" out of an order or soften a suggestion. This can backfire! You may come across as lacking power and possibly competence.

6. Can you take a good-natured ribbing? If a co-worker teases you, learn to laugh and practice quick comebacks that shows you are approachable and unflappable. Remember, it's not a good idea to become too sensitive. But, if you feel you are being ridiculed in the name of humor, take it up in private with the offending comedian.

Never use sarcastic humor or "private jokes" and use caution when introducing levity into a serious meeting or client presentation. But when the work pace is hectic and tension is building, humor may be just the thing to clear the air and re-charge everyone involved.

Can you poke fun at your company? Again, all the rules apply. But if you can find a way to spotlight a point of criticism with a joke, it may just lend strength to your commentary. Tone of voice will make or break you. For example: "We've got to stop meeting like this—we might actually get something done!"

Staying on the ball

It's time for women to get off the sidelines. The best way to score more points is to understand the rules and language of the sport of business. By understanding the dynamics of competition and relationships and how to use humor, we'll be good team players—able to have more fun and "hit it over the fence."

8

The balancing act: Integrating personal and professional

Say, for a moment, that your life sits on a balance scale. On one side is your career, your professional life. The other side holds all your family and personal obligations. What do you see? If you're a single woman building a new career, your scale will undoubtedly tip toward the professional. If you're a married woman with a young child, your scale may dip a bit more toward the personal. If you're the divorced mother of two school age children, watch out! Your scale may see-saw back and forth by the hour!

To complicate things even further, as you turn from side to side—playing employee, then care giver—your own personal needs often get lost in the balance. If you want to take some time to yourself, you may feel like the butcher who uses his finger to "cheat the scale."

Is striking a balance between the demands and rewards of both a personal and professional life really possible? It is essential.

A precarious process

To live a happy and fulfilling life, you need to keep some weight on either side of your life scale. But for women, that hasn't always been an option. In a flush of post-World War II prosperity, many women were eager to trade career aspirations for Mr. Right, a house in the suburbs and the life of a full-time wife and mother. With no professional accomplishments to offset the 24-hour-a-day job of serving the needs of a husband and family, many women felt vaguely unfulfilled.

Under the weight of personal obligations, one side of the scale can touch ground—leaving it vulnerable. Research later revealed that many of these women fell prey to depression and feelings of uselessness once the children left the nest.

Buoyed by the strides made by the women's movement in the 1960s and 1970s, we forged ahead—adding more professional responsibility to our full load of personal obligations. In order to pull it off, we had to believe we could become Superwomen. But with so much weight on both sides of the scale, the scale was in danger of breaking. Many professional wives and mothers suffered from feelings of guilt and burnout.

What's happening in the '90s? Young college women seem to be less inclined to "do it all." Many report they intend to avoid the Superwoman Syndrome by investing 100 percent of their energies in their careers. As a result, we may be back to square one. Without the rewards of a rich personal life to balance the demands of building a career, the scale can again take on a precarious tilt.

As you can see, professional freedom and enhanced career opportunities are only the beginning of a successful life—in which there is enough time for work, family and self. The hectic pace of our daily lives makes striking that balance more difficult than ever before. Changing circumstances are bound to tip the scale. But the more committed you are to bringing your life back into balance—recognizing the elements that throw it out of kilter—the happier and more effective person you'll be.

Setting priorities: A strategy

In his ground-breaking book called *The Seven Habits of Highly Effective People*, Stephen R. Covey outlines steps to achieving "Private Victories" as a prelude to "Public Victories." His premise is simple and powerful. Before we can concentrate on doing things right, we must first be sure we're doing the right things.

1. Make a plan. "Begin with the end in mind," Covey says. If you don't decide what kind of life you want to live, you may wake up to find yourself successful—but way off course from where you want to be. When you know where you're going, you can determine what your priorities are—and make sure your actions support them, every day. Covey suggests defining goals for each of your roles in key areas of your life, such as Manager, Friend, Wife, Mother.

2. Live the plan. Short-term actions are the foundation for long-term success. Your most important priorities should be at the top of your "to-do" list every day. But first, you should plan the week—scheduling "appointments" and commitments based on the goals for each role. In this way, Covey says, you'll "schedule your priorities, rather than prioritize your schedule."

3. "Sharpen the saw." You are your only resource. When the juice runs out and you run down—from illness or burnout—your plans will stall. Covey's final "habit," called "Sharpening the Saw," advises scheduling activities that support and protect your physical, mental and spiritual and social/emotional energies along with professional priorities.

Efficient or effective?

Is it possible to be efficient—and grossly ineffective? If you always seem to be "putting out fires"—reacting to urgent crises and deadline-driven projects—or allow yourself to get bogged down by busywork, you may be efficient. But as you busily cross those crises off your "to-do" list, is your adrenaline still pumping in anticipation of the next crisis?

The important things are not always the most urgent. In fact, devoting all your time and energy to the urgency of the moment doesn't leave time to make plans that might prevent future crises. Studies indicate that 80 percent of the results you desire will flow from 20 percent of your activities—especially if those activities involve preparation and relationship building. If you spend 100 percent of your efforts on managing crises, you will only continue traveling—very efficiently—in the same vicious circle.

Professional priorities

To be successful in the New Organization, you will have to combine professional expertise with interpersonal expertise.

American firms that fell behind in the global market have learned a hard lesson. Quality is key. Many companies have adopted quality improvement programs. To get ahead, you'll be expected to play an active role in increasing efficiency and quality. Continuing education and on-the-job training will be essential to maintaining expertise at every stage of your career.

More companies are recognizing collaboration as a positive replacement for no-holds-barred competition. Take a broad view of your company. How does your job relate to other jobs? How can you work with others to share in "bigger" successes? As a manager, how can you bring out the best in your staff? These are the questions high profile professionals will be asking themselves regularly in the future.

Taking care of (personal) business

What happens when your two worlds collide? If you're a mother, I know you can relate to the following scenario.

Midway through an executive meeting, I received an "important call from home." Voices were hushed. All eyes were on me as my eldest son, then in high school, asked whether the hitchhiker he picked up on the way home from school could stay the weekend because he had no place else to go! Appalled, yet unable to relay the full measure of my displeasure at that moment, I chose my words carefully.

"No, it is not appropriate for the gentleman to spend the night," I replied as pleasantly as I could—wondering what these "high rollers" must be thinking. "I will call you back in a half hour, when this meeting is over."

When I hung up the phone, I smiled calmly (over gritted teeth) and sighed "Children! Now...where were we?"

This type of interruption is a fact of life for most working mothers. Of course, I suggest establishing ground rules with your children regarding phone calls at work. And it may be wise to prearrange for some backup assistance from a nonworking neighbor or friend. But there will be emergencies. Simply handle each one as professionally as you would any other interpersonal interaction.

Personal priorities

To achieve balance at home, we can no longer "do it all." The rules must change. Many of us already ask for help from family members and outside service organizations. Innovative companies spring up daily to do those time-consuming tasks for you. No more Superwoman. Make that "Super Family." There's no reason why everyone can't chip in and do his or her part. When it isn't convenient for responsibilities to be shared, it's time to hire help.

Sources of support

Working parents need more options for competent, reasonably priced childcare and eldercare. Unfortunately, there is still plenty of room for improvement. More than 20 percent of employees who use childcare avoid jobs that require travel. Among management-level women, that figure shoots up to 40 percent! The answer lies in more flexible workstyles, including:

- New schedules, such as part-time work and work-at-home options.
- More generous leave for both parents.
- Transportation and day care for infants and school-age children, extending to after-school hours, summer and school vacations.
- Day care or assisted-living benefits for our aging parents and relatives.

Childcare: Hot topic or hot potato?

The United States lags far behind other industrialized nations in providing childcare programs for working parents. Some companies have addressed this issue and have built an experimental day-care site on the campus to test its success.

In many areas, "latchkey kids" are the norm. In others, day-care scandals are becoming common. Meanwhile, the cost of quality day care is becoming prohibitive for the average two-income family—not to mention single-parent households.

With no nationally endorsed alternative, many private companies are faced with picking up the slack if they want to attract and retain the very best people. Some larger organizations have already been successful in adding day care to their benefits portfolio. But the costs and logistics often make this difficult or simply not feasible for smaller businesses.

DuPont: One company's strategy

DuPont is one organization that has demonstrated its sensitivity to the demands of balancing work and family. In addition to training managers to be more sensitive and responsive to the needs of parents employed at all levels of the company, the company also has plans to:

- Reexamine career planning for managers to accommodate family demands.
- Introduce innovative work schedules.
- Lengthen parental leaves for both new mothers and fathers.
- Improve the availability and quality of childcare facilities.

Becoming a parent to our parents

It is already estimated that 5 million Americans spend some time caring for a parent every day. Within the next two decades, that number is expected to double. One 1985 study reported that 11 percent of working women, middle-aged and older, had to leave their jobs to care for an aging relative.

Even for the women who continue working, increased absenteeism, frequent phone calls and other problems continue to thwart productivity. Some larger organizations are stepping up to the issue. In late 1988, American Express and Proctor & Gamble became the first major U.S. corporations to offer employees and their families long-term care benefits such as coverage for nursing-home care.

Demographic studies predict that, by the year 2025, Americans over the age of 65 will outnumber teenagers by more than two to one! The effects of a "gray population" are expected to affect nearly every aspect of American culture and the American lifestyle. Surely, by then, older will be "better" for the majority. Until then, the agenda for eldercare should accelerate with each passing year.

That dirty word: Self-discipline

Half a century ago, researchers embarked on an ambitious study—with surprising results. Following the progress of nearly 300 men over the years after college graduation, researchers expected to find a correlation between scholastic performance and professional success. They found little, if any. They did some more digging. The one quality found consistently in each of the subjects who "made it big" was self-discipline. The ability to delay gratification while working diligently toward a defined goal is key. Dr. George E. Vaillant of Dartmouth Medical School, who now directs the project, describes it as "the capacity to postpone—but not forgo—gratification."

Remember the story of the rabbit and the hare? The "fast tracker" often expects too much too soon. When rewards and promotions are few and far between, this person is easily frustrated and can lose motivation. Be a turtle, instead. Keep the goal before you at all times, visualizing success in a finite way. Every step is progress, and every step has a bucketload of lessons. Savor each!

Success is a process, so take your time. Invest in a balanced life and you will be better equipped to make steady progress toward your goals. Self-discipline will help you go the distance.

9

The stages of your career: Branching out and moving up

Not along ago, most of us took it for granted that there was only one route to career success. College graduates, management hopefuls and aspiring members of the professions all lined up at the bottom of a ladder.

From the first rung, it was a straight and steady climb to the top. After completing a set of discrete steps, you expected to reach a level—often tagged with an age and sometimes a salary marker to let you know how well you were doing. Falling behind was cause for panic. Stepping out for schooling or to start a family often meant forfeiting your place on the ladder. There was only one way to go, ever upward.

Thankfully, the picture has changed.

Go climb a tree

Today, it makes more sense to put your ladder up to a tree. Now, rather than focusing simply on the rung ahead, you can often make better progress by venturing out to explore different branches of opportunity within your profession. Depending on your career aspirations, you may decide to make a lateral move that promises a better long-term payoff. By building skills and experience in a variety of areas, you'll develop agility and balance and create a stronger foundation for a career that can weather the test of changing times. A mix of experiences broadens you options.

Getting from here to there

Just as we all pass through stages of physical development from infant to adult, the stages of a career help us grow from novice to seasoned professional in a logical progression. Without perspective on the process, it's easy to feel "stuck" at one stage. The more awkward the stage, the more painful and endless it can seem. (Remember adolescence?)

Here's a brief life cycle.

Stage 1: Starting up

Everything seems fresh and new when you're just starting out. For now, the emphasis is on learning. If you're smart you'll become like a sponge—quickly soaking up every fact and skill you think you can use now or in the future.

This can be an emotional time. With no major failures or bad experiences to dampen your enthusiasm, you're "chomping at the bit" to make your mark. Your eagerness may come across as impatience. And in your zeal, you'll begin to make your first mistakes.

You may learn some difficult lessons. I did. At this stage, I found myself involved in resolving a conflict caused by a tyrannical vice president. Not only did this man manage to alienate his department through fear and intimidation, but he was blatantly carrying on an affair with a young employee!

After a number of management meetings, we agreed to recommend that the vice president attend counseling through the organization's employee assistance program. Within two months, he would be "eased out" of his position—and given a generous severance package to speed him on his way.

I was elated. So when one of the young men in the department, who wasn't privy to these plans, told me he was ready to quit to escape this vice president's recurring intimidation, I allowed my emotions to take reign over my professionalism. I told myself we couldn't risk losing a valuable employee over an issue that would soon be successfully resolved. It wouldn't be fair not to let him know what was going to happen. So I spilled the beans—in the "strictest confidence."

Well, you guessed it. In his youthful enthusiasm, this young man told someone else—who told the vice president! When I was called in for a lecture from my boss on the importance of confidentiality, I was completely embarrassed.

I didn't know I would one day look back and be grateful. That hard-won lesson molded my values. From that day on, I thought twice when I was tempted to act exclusively out of compassion for the underdog.

Mistakes don't have to be the end of the world—if you learn from them. Sometimes "failures" are only gentle messages in disguise. They may even tell you you're not cut out to pursue the direction you've chosen. In my case, my mistake confirmed my career path—but told me, in no uncertain terms, that I had a great deal to learn about organizational life. As a result, I was "sharper"—more focused than ever on achieving my goals and avoiding similar pitfalls.

Stage 2: The first plateau

The initial excitement has died down. You've tested your knowledge, skills and abilities within the context of a single job, and even tasted a little success. You're on your way, right? Then, why do you find yourself waking up in a cold sweat, grappling with a disturbing question.

"Is this all there is?" You may only have a vague sense of inertia, of being stuck in your present position. Perhaps opportunities have begun to narrow, people in leadership positions appear entrenched—and see you as entrenched in your current role. Don't panic. After all your energetic struggling, you've simply reached your first career plateau. If you aren't prepared, it can seem vast, endless.

Once you've achieved some success, you can rest, and take some time to look back—and look ahead. While it may feel like you're losing valuable time, take a breather from the hard work of climbing and concentrate on planning. What have you learned? What opportunities have you overlooked in your current job? Are you still headed in the right direction? What resources will you need for the next hard climb ahead.

You may decide to move on to another company, or to target another position in your own company. The time may be right to return to school for additional education. The important thing to remember is that plateaus don't go on forever. So take advantage of this time.

Stage 3: Rounding out

Challenge has returned. But now you've begun to expand your view of work to include other sources of satis-faction you may have repressed during the early years of your career. You may take up a hobby, lend a hand in a civic organization or decide to start a family. Celebrate.

You're becoming a well-rounded individual who will have more to contribute to work.

This can be a very satisfying period. Experiences you gain outside of work will help you look at your work from a new and different perspective. With more activities and interests, you'll begin to mark priorities and work toward goals in several different areas. In your growing maturity, you'll find a rich sense of responsibility and ac-countability.

Stage 4: Getting stuck, again

It was bound to happen. You may have hit your head on the "glass ceiling" within your company. Your industry may be struggling through an economic recession. Your geographical area may be depressed. You may have entered the job market too late in life. Whatever the reason for the present slowdown, it is probably out of your control. This time you're really stuck.

No way out? No easy way. By this time, you've acquired a "lifestyle"—that includes house payments, car payments, children, commitments! Even if you've been laid off, don't panic. It took you some time and dedicated energy to get to this point in your career. You owe it to yourself to take some more time to calmly reevaluate your new position. You will find you are not without choices or opportunities.

Get unstuck. What can you control? What do you realistically need to get moving again? An advanced degree or professional license or certification? How would your skills transfer to a more prosperous industry? Do you have enough experience to sell yourself as a consultant? A career counselor or headhunter might provide objective feedback.

Stage 5: Starting over

Not everyone will pass through this stage. Starting over may not be an option you even want to consider. If you're committed to the fast track, you may not see the opportunity. But it's important to know that there are many fresh options available to professionals—by choice or by chance.

Layoffs and downsizing can make starting over your *only* option. This can be traumatic if it happens without warning and if you haven't developed a contingency plan. Once the shock is over, why not consider this a blessing in disguise? What have you always dreamed of doing? Of course, you have to be practical. But, sometimes the most practical thing is to mesh your talents with the changing needs of the marketplace. The good news about a fluctuating business climate is that pockets of opportunity often turn up in abundance. Before you rush blindly into another similar job, you may want to take some time to consider finding a new niche or a new direction.

Like many women, you may find a second chance to do what you've always dreamed of doing as an entrepreneur. The time is ripe for setting up a home-based business. It is a trend that is here to stay. If you continue to work for a company, you may be able to negotiate a flexible schedule or do your current job at home—communicating via the "miracle" of modern tele-technology.

Stage 6: Making it

Success! You have the title, the salary, the status, the "Camelot" job. This is often a time when promotional opportunities abound and salary increases can come in rapid succession.

That twinkle in your eye. That burst of adrenaline when you arrive at work. This was worth waiting for! Enjoy it for all it's worth. As you've learned by now, this, too, will change with time.

At a time when your network is stronger and more expansive than it has ever been, you can work from your strength and connections. Scan the horizon for the next step. What opportunities are out there? What opportunities can you create for yourself? You have every reason to expect that you'll move on to something even more enriching.

Stage 7: Branching out

Once you've thrown the career ladder away, you have the freedom to explore. The more knowledge and experience you gain throughout your career, the more you can bring to any new venture as an executive or an entrepreneur.

A few words about the "glass ceiling"

"The glass ceiling in most companies is a lot lower than we thought it was," former Department of Labor Secretary Lynn Martin reports. "Too few women are getting the training they need to move up."

According to a recent article in *Fortune* magazine titled, "When Will Women Get To the Top?", we still have a long way to go. Our progress is likely to be slow—even for a growing number of "pioneers"—for a number of reasons. Chief among them, according to the CEOs polled for the article, was discrimination. Many CEOs confirmed that they are more comfortable passing the baton on to a "clone"—someone exactly like themselves.

Where does that leave women? About a third of the CEOs said they've noticed that women's careers often stall for lack of the kind support and mentoring networks men have long enjoyed. They also pointed to what they saw as a tendency for women to limit their own career paths by gravitating toward highly competitive industries, such as communications, or taking jobs in "soft" fields with little opportunity, such as administration.

The tide may be turning. Some organizations are beginning to invest in developing talented female middle managers for executive positions. In an increasingly competitive global economy, can any organization afford to discount half or more of its executive and management talent? Keep the faith and keep plugging.

Going out on a limb

If you've ever climbed a tall ladder, you know that the nearer you are to the top, the more it has a tendency to tip. Rather than put your career in peril with even a small change of circumstance, kick away the ladder! Over the long life of your career, the branches of your career tree will offer opportunity and stability. While it may sway with the winds of change, it will survive many storms. You can't lose, unless you choose not to climb.

10

Putting it all together: Your place in the landscape

So what does all this mean in the context of your career? As the artist of your own fate, only you can decide. The world of business is merely a canvas—primed with a number of the standard elements I've introduced to you in this book, such as business culture and discrimination. But the moment you add the first strokes of your own experience and knowledge, you personalize it. It is yours.

What will you make of your career?

There will always be factors you can't control. Business culture may alter some of your choices. Discrimination may repel even your best efforts. But simply by understanding the potential pitfalls, you can often avoid them.

Here's a recap of the key principles to help you blend your efforts into an integrated picture.

1. Think big. Look up from your desk often and take an active, rather than reactive, role in your department and your company or industry. Let your personal gifts and talents shine. Keep your skills sharp and your information up to date. Be aware of trends, and be ready to leap upon opportunities. Remember to think in macro rather than micro perspectives.

2. Become part of the *main*. No woman is an island. Invest in relationships with your boss, your peers and the many contacts you make as you network inside and outside your company or business. They will be among your most valuable assets as you build your career. Especially reach out to other women at all levels. By working together, we can all travel farther. In every relationship focus on a two-way exchange—of information, support, guidance and resources.

3. Join the team. Learn the language of business so you can become a key player on the team. Then play to win, using collaboration to create win-win, rather than win-lose situations.

4. Respect the landscape. The world of business has its own terrain, its seasons and its ever-changing climate. In this world, like any, success ultimately comes down survival of the fittest—in this case, the best and the brightest. Adapt to the environment, then show your stuff.

Benchmarks for continued success

The following inventories are designed to guide you through your own feedback. I encourage you to use them as tools to help you tune your efforts and realign your perspective throughout your career. Your first responses can provide a benchmark for your future progress. Check back every three to six months to see how you're doing, and to measure your progress toward your goals.

Culture inventory

Clues to a healthy environment

1. How would you describe the culture of your company or business?

Look back to earlier chapters for a refresher on the types of subtle and overt signals a company or business sends to customers and employees. Do your company's values match yours?

2. What trends are currently present in your industry? How has your company or business responded to them?

3. What changes has your company or business introduced over the past two years?

Were these changes made as a result of anticipating or reacting to other events? How have employees responded?

4. What is your company or business doing differently now than it was 5 or 10 years ago?

5. Is your company healthy today—with a clear vision for the future?

Does the management team operate with integrity in fulfilling its mission and goals?

Company profile inventory

Your company/business in a nutshell

Using the following "report card," check the one attribute in each of the following sets that best describes your company or business today.

Management philosophy

Structure and environment
❑ A. Hierarchical (many layers of management)
❑ B. Flat

Power base
❑ A. At the top
❑ B. In the teams

How power is used
❑ A. Collectively (often physical power)
❑ B. Collaboratively (mental power)

Behavior
❑ A. Superiority/rank
❑ B. Shared respect

Leadership
❑ A. Primarily white male
❑ B. Diverse

Reporting style
❑ A. Autocratic
❑ B. Democratic

Information
❑ A. Tightly controlled
❑ B. Available

Management perception of employees
❑ A. Cogs in the wheel
❑ B. Human capital

Promotion philosophy
❑ A. Based on seniority
❑ B. Based on competence

Compensation philosophy
❑ A. Based on rank
❑ B. Based on performance

Business philosophy

Primary focus
❑ A. Production
❑ B. The customer

❑ A. Quantity
❑ B. Quality

Orientation
❏ A. The product
❏ B. The process

Work style
❏ A. Production
❏ B. Systems

Primary resource investments
❏ A. Machinery
❏ B. Human "capital"

❏ A. Maintenance
❏ B. Innovation

Culture

Climate
❏ A. Formal
❏ B. Informal

❏ A. Solemn
❏ B. Energetic

Humor
❏ A. Caustic, punitive
❏ B. Free, spontaneous, not directed at individuals

Employee perception of benefits
❏ A. Entitlements
❏ B. Customized

Style of thinking valued
❑ A. Logical, fact-driven, linear thinking (Left-brain)
❑ B. Creative, non-linear, holistic (Right-brain)

Training philosophy
❑ A. A priority on the job
❑ B. Generalist

Guiding philosophy
❑ A. "The place makes the people."
❑ B. "The people make the place."

TOTAL:
A: _____
B: _____

If you checked a clear majority of A attributes, your company or business may be "stuck" in the Industrial Age. If you see more Bs, it has probably grown into the Information Age. Equal or nearly equal scores may indicate your company may still be in transition.

Role inventory
Take this job and love it?

How do you really feel about your current job? Is there a vague sense of dissatisfaction hanging over your efforts? Do you know what the next level is? Take the time to give each of the following questions your honest appraisal. Use a separate sheet of paper to record your thoughts in detail if necessary.

1. How important is work in my life?

2. How comfortable am I with the number of hours I spend doing my job?

3. Does my current job give me time to enjoy a satisfactory personal life?

4. What motivates me to work? Money? Challenge? Involvement with diverse people? The opportunity to learn and grow professionally? Something else?

5. How much money do I need to make?

6. In looking at my specific responsibilities:

Which tasks do I most enjoy performing?

What skills do I like to use?

What skills do I dislike using?

Which of these skills do I use most?

7. How would I objectively rate my job performance?

8. How would I rate the amount and level of responsibility and accountability I have?

9. How would I rate the amount and level of supervision that my boss exerts over my job?

10. What goals have I established for myself in this job?

11. **What skills do I need to develop in order to move ahead?**

12. **How far do I want to go in this company?**

13. **What is the next most logical job for me in this company?**

14. **What elements of my present job do I want to be part of my next job?**

15. What qualities in my current boss would I look for in my next boss?

16. How comfortable am I with management re sponsibilities?

17. How comfortable would I be with no management responsibilities in a technical role?

The professional network inventory

Building an active support system

Networking is a career-long investment that pays off in many ways. Assuming that you're already "out there"—actively pursuing professional relationships in your company or business, as well as in other professional organizations, how would you answer the following? (Circle the appropriate letter to indicate often (O), sometimes (S), never (N):

O S N Make an effort to building supportive and friendly professional relationships through networking.

O S N Plan my networking activities around my goals.

O S N Establish realistic timetables to achieve my goals.

O S N Consider networking as a full-time, ongoing job.

O S N Give as much as I get.

O S N Expect long-term rather than overnight, results from networking.

O S N Update my list regularly to include the names of new contact made through occasional cold calls.

O S N Have a file, notebook business card or other system to help me track responses and outcomes from my networking activities.

O S N Organize the name of my contacts in the most effective way—so that it is easy to update and purge names at least once a year.

O S N Have a clear understanding of the agenda and the group hosting each event I attend for networking.

O S N Maintain a positive and upbeat attitude.

O S N Focus on meeting individuals when I attend group events.

O S N Maximize my networking time by striking up conversations with people waiting to get into the event.

O S N Attach my name tag to the right lapel of my suit, so that I don't cover it up when I shake someone's hand.

O S N Make eye contact and smile when I meet new people.

The Smart Woman's Guide

O S N Seek out people standing alone, rather than try
to join in the conversation of a large group.

O S N Approach a table where only a few people are
seated, so it will be easier to join in the conversation.

O S N Have at least three "small-talk" questions on
tap at all times to make it easy to start conversations with new people.

O S N Ask open-ended questions that draw people
into conversation.

O S N Check in with contacts I've made through
networking events every few months to maintain contact and offer support in a non-
threatening manner.

O S N Call only at appropriate times, as a common
courtesy to other professionals.

O S N Keep my promise to send articles or fulfill
special requests by referring to notes I've made
on the back of business cards.

O S N Send copies of newspaper or magazine
articles—along with a personal note—to
contacts who might be interested.

O S N Respect each contact's personal wishes when
using his or her name or making a referral.

Notes

Notes

Notes

Notes

Notes

Notes

The best is up ahead

So, this is an end—but it is also a beginning. I hope you'll use the information in this book to improve your performance and your prospects. But I hope you'll go on learning.

Building a successful and rewarding career is a rich and fulfilling process that demands the very best you have to give. So, above all, I hope you've gained a strong sense of your own personal power. In the face of everything else, it can be the deciding factor in your own success.

My parting gift is my very best wish for your brilliant career!

Epilogue

As you leave work some clear fall evening, look up at the sky. You can almost depend on seeing the silhouette of a flock of geese, heading south for the winter in their characteristic "V" formation. In the beautiful symmetry of nature's plan, there's a lesson for every one of us learning to be part of a professional team.

Each goose in the V "lifts" the bird behind in the updraft of air it creates by flapping its wings. Any goose that falls out of formation immediately feels the increased resistance of trying to go it alone and returns. When the leader tires, it rotates back in the wing to let another goose fly point. All along the way, the geese honk encouragement to their traveling partners.

But when one of the formation becomes sick, or is wounded by a hunter's gunfire, two companions also fall out to protect the fallen bird until it is able to fly again. When these birds continue on, they may join another passing formation if they're unable to catch up with the original group.

Over the course of a long journey, the "V" formation has a cumulative effect—the flock can travel 71 percent farther together than one of the geese could travel on its own.

The Smart Woman's Guide

We may not have the built-in instinct for teamwork a goose has, but it's difficult not to appreciate its wisdom.

As part of a group that shares a common purpose, we can arrive at our goals more quickly and easily than would be possible alone. Mutual encouragement and support keeps us going.

Over the course of a lengthy project, we can share difficult tasks and "lift" each other through our combined efforts. Over the course of a career, we can reduce resistance and maximize our distance by building professional relationships. If we've invested wisely and well, we should be able to expect our colleagues to come to our aid if we falter.

What does this have to do with women? We need to learn collaboration, shared power and trust. Women must help other women so that we don't fall behind the flock. We must inspire and encourage other women. At any moment in our personal lives, we may not be leading the pack, but may be following a strong and competent leader. Our time will come and we must each be ready.

By now, you should know that the sky is the limit. It will be a long journey—but we can go the distance if we travel together. Godspeed.

Index